Lonely Project

Surviving and thriving in the world of change management

Tales of the best and worst ways to navigate one of business's most challenging environments by the people who've been there

Nick Waugh

www.nickwaugh.co.uk

Copyright 2008 Nick Waugh

First published in Great Britain in 2008 by View Books

The rights of Nick Waugh as author of the work has been asserted by him in accordance with the Copyright, Designs and Patents Act 1988

Cover design and branding by Objective Ingenuity
www.objectiveingenuity.com

All rights reserved. No part of this publication may be reproduced, stored in a retrieval system, or transmitted, in any form or by any means without the prior written permission of the publisher, nor be otherwise circulated in any form of binding or cover other than that in which it is published and without a similar condition being imposed on the subsequent purchaser.

ISBN 978-0-9559248-0-4

www.lonelyproject.com

Contents

	Foreword	5
	Introduction What's this book all about?	9
1	Vision Why are we doing this?	19
2	Planning Preparation is everything	39
3	Design Rubbish in, rubbish out	61
4	Delivery Where heroes are made	79
5	Readiness What's the customer say?	97
6	Realisation Was it worth it?	113
7	Governance Controls with teeth	129
8	People We really do like change	143
9	Communication Shoot the spin doctors	165
10	Review What we did right	185

Appendices

A	10 mildly interesting statistics	203
B	10 ways to tackle change resistance	207
C	10 reasons why I failed	213
D	10 reasons to worry	219
E	10 ways to kill an idea	225
F	10 successful behaviours	231
G	20 tips for a successful meeting	237
H	20 questions	243
I	10 useful references	249
J	10 facts about the author	253

Foreword

I recently took a trip to Africa, a continent I have visited many times but to a region that was new to me. My aim was to see a number of specific sights, engage in a new culture through meeting indigenous people, and take some spectacular photos. I had planned my route through the country and pre-booked accommodation, but had left enough time in my schedule to 'free-wheel' within a fixed time period. My first opportunity to do this was shortly after arrival. I checked into a basic hotel that was clean and had essential facilities but certainly encouraged me to leave it. So I went for my first walk, early evening.

The sunset behind a skyline of new modern concrete blocks and corrugated roofs of a shantytown was quite striking. New and old, rich and poor, were living in unison. I wasn't sure if this was a city in transition or whether the extremes were going to be accentuated further over time. I headed for the market where you can usually rely on there being bustling activity and lots of opportunity for colour and life in photos. I always feel a confence boost when I've got my first few great photos under my belt, which encourages me to be a bit braver in latter parts of the journey. Something I completely underestimated and had forgotten about was the amount of hassle I was going to get.

From the first step I made into the market area I was surrounded by local people trying to get my attention. Old and young tried taking me to their family shop or offering discount on products I didn't want, or offering their services as a guide, or taxi on a horse and cart, or some illegal beer, drugs… an endless barrage of selling and begging. One young man who spoke perfect English offered me hassle free shopping whilst physically dragging me towards his market stall where he sold pipes. Having only been in this environment for a few hours I was a bit overwhelmed by all the attention. I strode purposefully through the market trying to fend off the attention I was getting. Stopping to look was not an option and taking photographs was even more difficult. Even if I could stay steady enough without being knocked off balance, I would be constantly asked for money, even for taking a picture of tomatoes. After half an hour I returned to my room, exhausted, adrenalin pumping and heart racing. I sat, slumped, thinking, "What an earth happened there?"

I should have been prepared for this and I should have had some tactics. I experienced it many times before. I knew what to do about it. A similar thing happened on my last African trip and I learned how to say no, what phrases would make them give up, what body language to use in the absence of mutual vocabulary. In really tough situations I would hire a guide for a few pounds and he would keep all the others away. They respected that the local had 'got the gig' and did much of their bartering with him. I was free to take photos, even the ones of elderly people who thought their spirit would be captured (when offering only a few pennies this often seemed less important to them). When shopping, there is definitely a set of rules you adopt to get the best deal, such as starting outrageously low, showing no interest in something you really want, walking away if the negotiation stalls. All these things would result in a positive experience, a good engagement with the culture, and a great set of photos. So why didn't I do what I, or a number of other experienced travellers, already knew.

I started my journey without thinking, without calling on all of my experience and without a guide. The guide could have been a person, but there is an amount of risk here as they usually have their own agenda (I remember spending a long time in a pepper field in Borneo because it was owned by my guide's brother). More reliable is a reminder of past experiences. How useful it would have been to have a few lines on my learning from previous trips when encountering each stage of a journey. Even more useful would be the learning of hundreds of people who have made a similar journey and had similar aims. Of course these types of travel guides do exist and have contributions from experienced travellers and are kept current by a growing travel community.

There are a lot of books on business transformation, change management and programme management. There are even more on project management. In the main, they are based on the latest models, tools, and methods and are targeted at learning something new. Lonely Project is different. It is a guide that helps people through the programme change journey based on the experiences of others. The guide tells stories of professionals who have made the journey many times before and are still learning from treading new and proven paths.

If after reading this book you would like the additional value of a personal guide to help plan or execute a stage of your change programme journey please visit **www.lonelyproject.com**. You can also become a contributor to future Lonely Project guides through posting your own experiences.

Introduction
What's this book all about?

Introduction
What's this book all about?

Why I wrote this book

I have been involved in change programmes for over 20 years. Compared with many industries it is young and evolving, which may give us comfort from the disturbing failure rate. Whichever statistic you choose to quote, it is widely perceived that more change programmes fail than succeed, whether it be a total write-off, an over-run in costs and time, or a shortfall in benefits. This has frustrated me for many years as I know the amount of effort that goes into delivering change programmes and there is rarely a corresponding amount of recognition.

So I thought I would do some research on how to increase the chances of success, based on real people's experience, not theory.

There are many good books on change management theories, methods, models and tools, and I have read a lot of them. Many of them seek to introduce something new to improve the change management process and many are a vehicle for selling products and services. I have found this material useful and interesting, but when I look back at the times I have learned the most it is directly from people's experience; the little sound bites of advice, the war stories, the amusing anecdotes and the tales of moments when it all went horribly wrong. That's what this book is all about, the invaluable experiences that would have been so useful had they been known before embarking on a change programme.

Having referred to these stories and my collection of notes during my own programmes, I decided to share them with others. I hope that in some way this will increase the success rate of future change programmes.

Why you should read this book

If you don't have to do a large, long, complex change programme, it could be argued that you shouldn't, as statistically you will fail. But sometimes it is absolutely the right thing to do. This book will provide you with some guidance, wherever you are in the change cycle, from programme start-up mode through to benefit realisation.

As a leader of change, just imagine if you had a lower cost, more manageable change portfolio that always delivered benefits that were enabling strategic objectives… over and over again. Delivering change programmes can be a great competitive advantage or a high cost burden on people and profits.

The content of this guide is based purely on peoples' experience, at all levels, from CEO to administrator, from consultant to cleaner (yes, I did ask the cleaners for their observations when they were trying to do their job among a lot of tired people and empty pizza boxes). At times there are references to models, theories, methods and tools but the promise is that it's all related to real experiences of real people.

The target audience for this book is a multitude of different programme roles, from sponsor to project manager, and for all levels of experience, from programme veteran to project virgin. The guide is mainly about large change programmes that include multiple projects. It's not about how to manage individual projects, although there are some experiences and themes that are relevant to project management and smaller changes. The emphasis is on managing change that will have significant and lasting positive impact on an organisation. Inevitably, there are some systems development references but there is equal value to anyone responsible for a function going through major change involving customers, colleagues, processes and technology.

The handbook is not intended to replace training or education, but to compliment formal methods of learning. It is an easy to read manual of key learning points for improving your chances of success.

How to read this book

The composition of the handbook is a mix of lists, quotes, diagrams and stories. Sometimes all of these styles are used to get across key points in different ways. This helps understanding and adapts to many different learning styles. The book is designed to be flexible in its reading in that you may want to read it cover to cover to absorb all the experiences at once or you may wish to visit a section based on a particular challenge or issue you are facing.

Each chapter has a story, some analysis, and refers to models and tools. The use of a story sets the scene from a real life experience. This is followed by some analysis of the story's learning points and extraction of best and worst practice. The chapters include solutions using new or existing models and tools. I hope you forgive the occasional digression from a chapter's subject. When a thought came into my head it is usually relevant in some way due to the nature of links and overlaps between sections.

Some of the chapters could lend themselves to sequential reading such as following the change life cycle from vision through to realisation. An important point is to acknowledge that some sections are relevant all the way through the cycle, such as governance and communication. The diagram below shows the sequential sections and the 'wrapped' sections.

The purpose of the diagram is to show a structure for the ten sections of the book and is not meant to follow a methodology. The arrows suggest that after each section it may be worth revisiting an earlier one, as they are all linked and, although experiences are aligned to a primary section, they pan multiple ones.

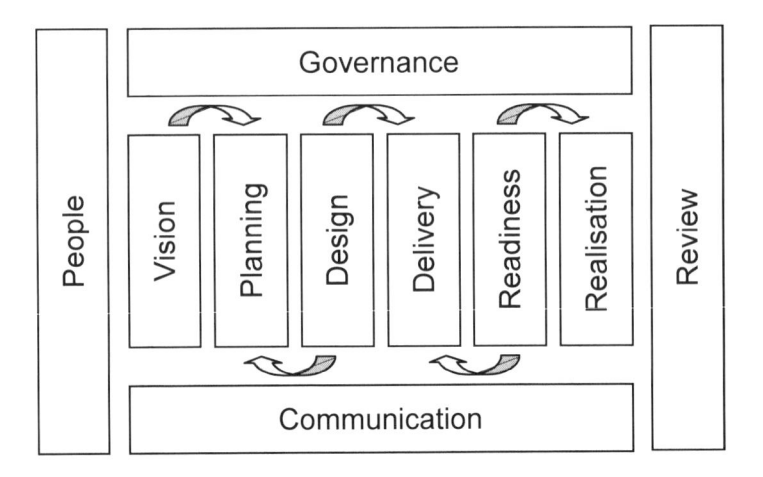

```
┌──────┬─────────────────────────────────────────────┬──────┐
│      │                 Governance                  │      │
│      │   ⤻         ⤻         ⤻                     │      │
│ People│ Vision │Planning│Design│Delivery│Readiness│Realisation│ Review │
│      │   ⤸         ⤸                              │      │
│      │               Communication                 │      │
└──────┴─────────────────────────────────────────────┴──────┘
```

My experience, and one supported by many contributors to this book, is that one of the key mistakes made in change programmes is to ignore the need to continually focus on all aspects of a programme. For example, if you think you've communicated the vision at the beginning of the programme and are able to tick the box, then you're wrong. It requires constant re-iteration throughout the programme and re-visiting and amending along the journey. This also applies to doing regular reviews, continually assessing the make up of the teams, and monitoring the effectiveness of the governance.

A final thought on how to read this book is that I believe it's not a one off guide that is ever finished. I have kept it by my side since it's early unpublished version and am amazed by how many times I am about to make the same mistake. We all have natural strengths and weaknesses and it is so useful to have a reminder to guide you through things that you're more likely to forget. Many of the experiences in this book are obvious and could even be deemed common sense. That is exactly the point, all the contributors to this book have been educated, trained and have several projects under their belt, but have often used the phrase "if only someone had reminded me of that beforehand".

Whichever way you use this guide I hope you extract some learning or a reminder of something you had forgotten. If you change just one thing in your programme that increases your chance of success, then it's been worth the read.

Information Sources

When first considering writing this handbook I thought that in order to give it credibility I would have to obtain data from hundreds of people with experience of hundreds of projects in big multi-national organisations from different sectors. So that's what I did, and ended up with thousands of years of experience. As the data started to pile up and the interviews were conducted, trends started to appear very early. On reflection, a sample size of about 20 would have been enough to draw some genuine conclusions. But what I would have missed out on is the richness of expressions, humour and at times drama that people put into their responses to my questions.

The experience was extracted from a number of sources of input:

Interviews. I have conducted formal sessions with programme team members and also coffee machine chats with people on the periphery. I spoke with people who were delivering and people who were receiving the change. I asked questions of technology suppliers, strategy consultants, behavioural psychologists and even actuaries (no offence!).
Questionnaires. I devised a simple questionnaire with open questions to allow for freethinking. It was harder to analyse and interpret than a standard multiple choice style questionnaire but

through careful targeting, the response rate was high. The quality of response was superb. There was a mixture of fact, story, reflection, perception, and at times raw emotion. In order to provide a more statistical approach to programme experience I also issued a longer but multiple choice style questionnaire. Details of these questionnaires are in appendix H.

PIR and PER. Otherwise known as Post Implementation Review and Phase End Review. Not everyone conducts this formal approach to reflection and learning and there are different degrees of depth and breadth in the content. I strongly believe in their use; during a programme to improve the chances of success of later phases and at the end of the programme to learn for the next one. In fact, an alternative title for this book was going to be 'The Ultimate PIR' (but it's a bit nerdy). The source here was two-fold; attending as many as I was allowed to as an observer or even participant, and receiving as much of the documented output as I could.

Personal Experience. I have tried to keep the experiences as true to the source as possible, at times even when I don't wholly agree. But when it comes to summaries and strong advice then this is based on my analysis of the information and on my own experience.

There is clearly a passion for the subject of change programmes and a huge desire to make programme management a more successful profession. It is certainly fraught with risk and danger and the statistics don't always make pleasant reading. But the memorable personal experiences seem to drive people to do more and more change programmes and attempt to do them better. There has been a great willingness to support this book and an equal keenness to receive the output.

Most people and organisations didn't want their identity revealed and so obviously I have respected that. They certainly wouldn't have been so forthcoming with the failures if they were personally associated with them.

I'd like to thank everyone for their time, whether it was in conducting a detailed interview, answering questionnaires, or forwarding documentation to me. I hope you find it an enjoyable read and you obtain as much value in reading the book as I have had in producing it.

1

Vision
Why are we doing this?

Topics include:
- Engaging with the vision
- Programme selection
- Enterprise architecture
- Change categorisation
- Aligning the vision
- The business case

1: Vision
Why are we doing this?

If you don't know why you're doing something, you are very unlikely to fully meet its objectives. This applies to everyone involved in a change programme and only with collective and personal vision will it be a success in everyone's eyes.

Yet another leader to undermine
by an IT analyst

After years of stability, comfort and very little major change I found myself in a room with the latest director who thought he was going to change the world. I'd seen them come and go and no-one had really succeeded. Most of us played lip service to the latest evangelism and waited until it faded away and we could return to our normal lives again.

The first speech was similar to others, although he was younger, fresher and really seemed to mean what he was saying. Poor guy, I thought, he'll be as disillusioned as the rest of us within a few months. He clearly outlined the ambition of the company, his new department, and spent an unusual amount of time on cultural change. The usual cynics started their trouble and cockily almost set a challenge for him to succeed. As usual they would be behind the projects and tangible goals, but no-one was going to change their behaviour and they were going to retain total control of their own destiny. Then at the end of the meeting, having listened to a quite forthright exchange of views on cultures and ambition, the bombshell was dropped. We were going to have to do some things that were right out of our comfort zone.

We were split into teams on the basis of where we were sitting. This was immediately concerning, as we were not with all our friends and close colleagues. Some of the people were from different disciplines and we hardly knew them. It was a smart move to mix us up and also do it in a way that was obviously not contrived and planned in advance. It was transparent and everyone could see the first example of the way things would be different (in the past we'd have spent weeks designing the perfect combinations of teams to try and satisfy everyone). The teams then had 3 minutes to choose a leader. Again, quite uncomfortable as usually this would have been the most senior person and everyone could blame the management for the awful things to come. Then it got even worse as the outline of a workshop was briefed. Having heard the new director's vision for our department we were to prepare a performance that embodied the new vision and we were given a small budget for any props we would need. End of brief! Every question, many with a hint of panic in the voice, was met with "that's up to you" or similar response. We had 4 weeks.

The location for the workshop was a zoo. Usually it would be a stuffy hotel with PowerPoint presentations and scripts to an audience in theatre style seating. This was an empty room, totally empty except for the props that were brought along. The day was more structured than I imagined. Each performance was given and then discussed. We all had to vote on which performance best represented the vision and so we spent a long time discussing the key points of the vision, over and over again. Clever, I thought. Even if we didn't buy it, we were certainly going to understand it by the end of the day.

The results were quite extraordinary. Looking back, I never thought I would see certain people singing, acting, doing circus acts, dressing up, and above all laughing so hard they were crying. Those that didn't put the effort in were in the minority and I know some of them wished they had 'gone for it' a bit more. Every person had to be involved so it was truly a team effort and everyone had to go through the same embarrassment. The creativity was tremendous and many hidden talents were surfaced. We had Rolf Harris, Jerry Springer, Chas'n'Dave, Agatha Christie, University Challenge, Teletubbies, Billy Smarts Circus, and many more local and company jokes. The room looked incredible at the end as all the props were displayed on walls, worn, or left in heaps on the floor. It was also filmed, which was rather scary at first but after a while people forgot about the camera. At the end of the day we had food and drinks and lots of banter. Unusually, most people stayed until they were asked to leave.

Some people refused to get involved and didn't turn up. This wasn't frowned upon at all but they were made to feel really left out as nothing much else was talked about for weeks. The film and stills from the day were regularly played back in meetings, project reviews, and every time we needed a reminder of what the vision was all about (or needed a good laugh).

The successes were many. Total transparency of team selection and freedom do what we wanted. We waited for the hidden agenda but it didn't come. Everyone had the opportunity to express the vision in their own way, personalizing it. We spent weeks of preparation and a whole day reflecting on the vision, but in many different ways. The event was very different for us and signalled a change with action rather than just words. There was no repercussion for abstainers. All this was new and generated excitement and a buzz. We saw a different future, created by us, and had already started to experience it.

The story demonstrates a great way of starting to engage people in a significant change. There are many learning points that can be extracted from the story:

- The focus on cultural or people change before systems, process and organisation is refreshing for people and is likely to engage them sooner.
- Doing something different from the norm will excite or frighten people but it will definitely grab their attention. Cynics will not be able to easily identify the floors.
- Mix people up away from their cliques if you have a resistance to listening or involvement in a new vision. This reduces the influence and power base of the cynics.
- Transparency and simplicity work well when presenting new ideas and plans. Complexity is less easily understood and can result in suspicion or even re-creation of the truth.
- Repeat the vision over and over again. Find different ways to say the same things. Encourage people to express the vision in a way that means something to them. A link with a personal vision is a powerful method of creating advocacy.
- Provide a framework for expressing the vision but encourage creativity. There is no limit to people's imaginations once they start to enjoy the freedom. They will surprise themselves and others.
- Total group participation should be the aim. Everyone should be treated the same and encouraged to get involved but should have a choice as to how. Allow for different personality types in the manner in which people reflect their interpretation of the vision.

The importance of a clear and attainable vision in a change programme is supported by John Kotter, a renowned expert in leadership. Kotter found that after researching 100 companies, less than 15 of them were successful in their transformation programmes. He describes eight mistakes commonly made during change. Three of these mistakes are directly related to the vision and others are indirectly related. Creating a vision, communicating a vision and empowering people to act on the vision are critical to successful change.

Most leaders under-communicate their change vision by a factor of 10. They tend to use repetitive vehicles for delivering the communication, such as speeches and memos. They do not do anything new or inventive to express a change and therefore they are role modelling old behaviours rather than taking the opportunity to show they are changing too. People observe the actions and behaviours of their leaders and most importantly their direct manager. They won't change unless they are given 'permission' to.

In addition to having a clearly understood vision it is important to have well defined, short-term, attainable goals that are stepping-stones to achieving the long-term vision. A frequent mistake of leaders is to make the vision too grand and distant, making it difficult for people to connect their individual roles or actions to the vision. The vision needs to be reachable which means having a good balance between short-term goals and long-term strategy. This helps map a journey to achieving the vision from a personal and collective point of view. The table below shows a simple relationship between short-term goals and vision.

Vision \ Goals	Long	Short
Strong	Unattainable Change	Sustainable Change
Weak	Stagnation	Tactical Change

If the vision is clearly defined and has aligned, achievable short-term goals then there is a higher chance of achieving sustainable change. A clear vision with long-term goals is likely to waiver as there would be minimal evidence of success on a long journey. Goals without a vision will achieve change but often directionless and changes are likely to be undone or frequently superseded.

The experiences of the people contributing to this book support the view that the vision is one of the most critical elements of change.

Programme selection

The stage before even the visioning of a programme is to ensure the right programmes are being done. Most investment portfolios have a finite budget and therefore getting the maximum return from each programme and the whole portfolio is extremely important. One of the biggest difficulties organisations have during the life of a programme is cancelling it and writing off large sums of money. Sometimes this is because circumstances have changed (see appendix D, 10 reasons to worry) but sometimes because it wasn't the right programme to start with. The funnel diagram below helps illustrate this point.

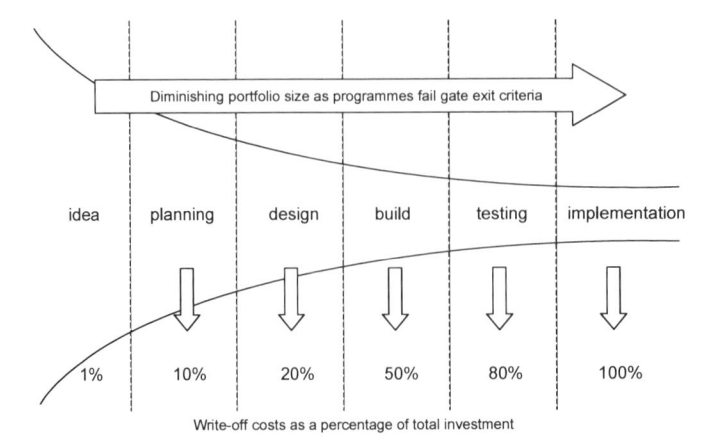

idea	planning	design	build	testing	implementation
1%	10%	20%	50%	80%	100%

Diminishing portfolio size as programmes fail gate exit criteria

Write-off costs as a percentage of total investment

The stages of a programme may change and the percentages will vary; the numbers in the diagram are rough averages across a selection of programmes that were cancelled.

The two key messages are simple, but rarely followed:

1. The later you realise your programme should be cancelled or significantly amended, the more expensive it will be.
2. A programme should be selected once at initiation and then re-selected at every stage of its cycle to assess its independent value, and its value relative to the current portfolio and new ideas. The use of exit and entry criteria at gates between stages is a good practice to adopt.

One of the reasons that the failure rate of programmes is so high is that many should have been shut down or modified earlier in their life cycle than they have been. There are many models, processes and tools to do programme selection at the initiation stage and some of them work well. Some organisations make investment decisions by committee supported by sophisticated scorecards. Others have a more dictatorial approach by their CEO. Both are valid mechanisms but it's important for buy-in that everyone knows which mechanism they are using.

The diagram below is something similar to that drawn by a rather cynical and fed up programme office who were facilitating programme selection sessions with their executive team. The chart on the left is the programme investment category scorecard that was used to evaluate and compare programmes at the selection stage. The chart on the right is what happened in practice.

The 'CEO wants it' category is perfectly valid but should be transparent and not go through the process of scoring 12 other categories and trying to make it fit retrospectively.

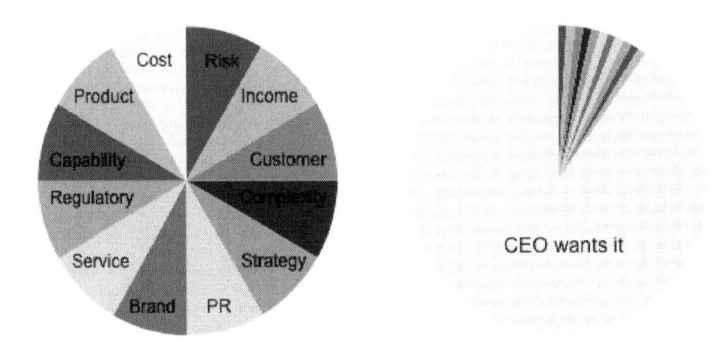

Enterprise architecture

There is no right way to determine which programmes should be in your portfolio, but there are certainly some more sophisticated, and more likely to produce the right areas for change, than others. The Zachman model of enterprise architecture is a framework that helps you move from business strategies and goals through to defining what change is required to deliver them.

> *"You wouldn't significantly modify your house without an architect, so why try changing a business without one?"*
>
> *enterprise architect*

The key output to do this is enterprise architecture, or a model of all or part of your business. I could write a lot of pages on this but would add little additional value from what you could read on the Zachman framework website. For large and complex change I would recommend using a consultancy to help you with developing an enterprise architecture. For example, Altus are a consultancy with a proven record of saving companies money and enabling business strategy through focusing on the right areas of change.

I've worked with CEOs who have loved and hated enterprise architecture and the building of target operating models. One of the key reasons for under-valuing the output is the lack of evidence of financial benefit produced by some architects. It can be done. Like most investments there should be a business case for doing the work and a review of benefits at the end. Given the number of projects that fail to meet cost and benefit targets, I'd suggest there is room for more effort at the initiation stage.

When is a programme a programme?

This is a question worth answering before embarking on a programme to establish the best delivery vehicle for the change. I once delivered a pep talk to a deflated change manager who was responsible for all change in the organisation. He was concerned about how to motivate his team who were being messed about by changing priorities and the need for unreasonable fluidity in his plans. He was managing all change in a structured and disciplined way with strict controls and methodology. The issue was that not all change should be managed in this way. I drew the diagram below on a white board.

The first point was to demonstrate how central the change function was to delivering the strategic objectives of the organisation. The second point was to use the diagram to determine change complexity and what was the most appropriate delivery vehicle (programme or other).

Being the centre of all the organisations key activities should be seen as a positive opportunity. Also the amount of demand should be seen as a measure of their potential value. The organisation simply couldn't progress without them. But it wasn't seen as positive because his customers were frustrated with perceived bureaucracy and under delivery. The change function was seen as a constraint to business objectives rather than a key enabler. There were three problems. Firstly, there was over-engineering of small and simple change, or 'project-itis'. Secondly, there was a lack of a funnelling process to reduce the demand to the most valuable activities and eliminate the 'noise'. Lastly, there was little transparency of the process and outputs to the stakeholders. Let's deal with the first problem here (the other two are covered later in this chapter).

A crude method of determining complexity is to look at the number of key stakeholders (in the outer wheel of the diagram) and the number of key suppliers (in the inner wheel). The higher number, the more control and structure required. To make this more visual, if you draw a line between all the relationships of stakeholders and suppliers it will show how much need there is for a middle layer of facilitation and control. If the wheel looks like a Spirograph picture then you need a programme.

The diagram is only a simplified example and most organisations will have many more stakeholders and suppliers to consider. Of course this is not the only indication of complexity but if you add scale of investment and benefit then you start to build a convincing picture. Having determined complexity the next question is how we treat the delivery of the change. The diagram below is a good example of the delivery vehicles for change.

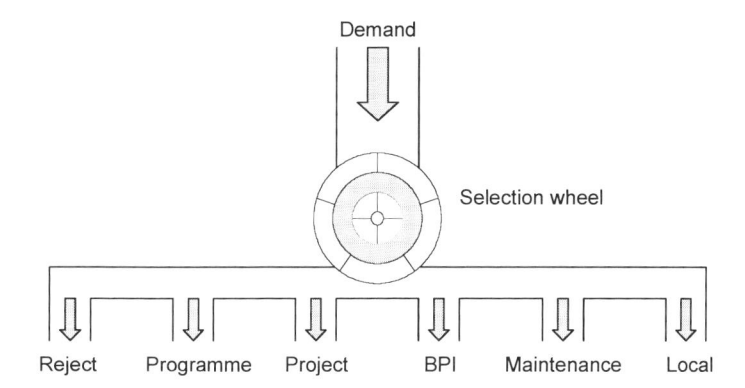

```
                    Demand
                      ⇩

                  ╱─────╲
                 │ Selection wheel
                  ╲─────╱
       ┌──────┬──────┬──────┬──────┬──────┐
       ⇩      ⇩      ⇩      ⇩      ⇩      ⇩
    Reject Programme Project BPI Maintenance Local
```

How the change function is organised will determine where the change is managed and delivered. The key point is they will be managed with a different degree of control, structure, methodology, monitoring and risk management. The descriptions of each delivery category are here for completeness, the key message being in the reject category.

Reject. A really important category in order to save time and money in the future. Ideas are rejected for many reasons and often a key reason is timing e.g. market conditions, current strategy, capability, and regulatory climate. Therefore as internal or external factors change, ideas can become relevant again. Also, with change of personnel it's amazing how many times the same idea gets raised. When this occurs it saves a lot of effort if the assessment history can be quickly recalled. With credibility the idea can then be quickly re-assessed. So many good ideas are lost because people respond with "oh, we looked at that before and it didn't stack up". Well maybe it will now. This is probably a good time for a bit of digression and a look at something amusing and so true to many of our experiences. Appendix E lists 10 ways to kill an idea. I'm sure we've all been guilty of at least one of them.

Programme. My definition of a programme is a collection of projects that are delivering an integrated change and have linked benefits that are aligned to a single vision. Programmes are often transformational and involve change to people, process and technology. They are also typically large in scale and complexity, requiring high levels of structure, control and monitoring. This book is mainly concerned with this type of change.

Project. A project can have delivery dependencies and benefit links with other projects but can usually be delivered in isolation. The change will be of medium size and complexity and have a stand-alone objective. Typically there are more projects ongoing in an organisation than any other change because of the variety of controls and monitoring available. This flexibility and visibility makes it ideal for a change, whether it is people, process or technology.

BPI (Business Process Improvement). Also known by other names and acronyms and can also be considered a project. But typically without technology changes, BPI projects can be quicker and simpler, just focussing on the process. They are supported by different methodologies and tools (such as Lean or Six Sigma) but there are many overlaps with programmes and sharing of good practice, such as benefit management, monitoring and review. BPI projects can be varied in size, complexity and can be treated as stand-alone projects or as part of a programme. Many organisations have a separate BPI function and a healthy competition between the return on investment (ROI) for each type of project. After only 6 months after set up, one organisation were delivering a higher ROI from their BPI team than any other change vehicle.

Maintenance. These are small changes that are low risk and should be performed outside of complex project and programme governance. They are critical to keeping an organisation fluid and flexible in its change capability. Most organisations have a budget for maintenance changes, with its own benefit target and prioritisation forum. With good systems architecture and business design in place, some of these small changes can deliver the highest returns.

Local. In my IT days I would never have advocated such a category as the 'do-it-yourself' type change in local departments (e.g. Marketing, Finance, MI, Risk). They can often become a big IT headache. Now I firmly believe there is a valid place for local change providing it is the right kind of change. The key is to have no need for integration, or dependency on other systems and processes. The control and governance discipline needs to be there, although with a lighter touch which can be managed in the department. Visibility of the changes must be available to the project office or change department so that the overall change calendar can be managed. A change calendar is an excellent vehicle for communication to all colleagues and ensuring that the amount of change and any conflicts can be managed. One danger of local change is when it grows into a cottage industry and there is a risk that the solutions cannot be supported or maintained. The change function needs to have oversight of these changes to assess risk and advise on acceptance levels.

Back to my pep talk with the disillusioned change manager. He re-organised his function into three departments, each managing a different type of change. His customers saw quicker throughput, more flexibility, lower costs, more control and greater appreciation. The teams were given new skills, became experts in new fields and had clear career path options.

Aligning the vision

Before we take a further look at some experiences and best practice regarding this element of change I think it is worth positioning the vision in the change architecture of a business.

The static nature of the pyramid in the diagram below is appropriate to describe the change architecture, but it can incorrectly imply a start and an end to a process.

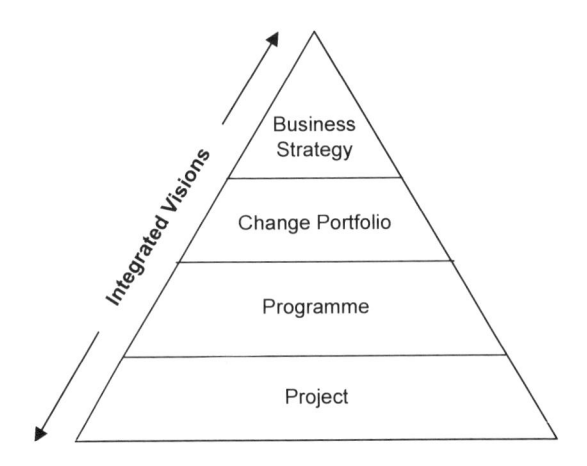

```
                    /\
                   /  \
                  / Business \
                 /  Strategy  \
                /──────────────\
               /                \
              / Change Portfolio \
             /────────────────────\
            /                      \
           /      Programme         \
          /──────────────────────────\
         /                            \
        /          Project             \
       /────────────────────────────────\
```
Integrated Visions

One of the key mistakes businesses make is to produce a programme and/or portfolio once a year and never revisit its relevance to an ever-changing set of strategic priorities, key performance indicators (KPIs), external market changes, and regulatory requirements. Critical to keeping the programme relevant is the "should we still be doing this?" review. A similar exercise should take place for projects within a programme based on their continuing value to the business case. When the answer is that the change is no longer relevant or isn't going to deliver enough value, then the business must be brave to take the tough decision and cancel or redesign the programme and incur potentially large write offs. If the portfolio is focussed on delivery rather than benefit, then the wasted money and damage to credibility will be large. The vision can be best friend or worst enemy in this regard.

It is this constant challenge of programmes against business goals that keeps the change portfolio relevant and manageable, delivering tangible benefits and enabling strategic objectives.

The Business Case

The key document for defining and measuring success of a change programme is the business case, with its detailed cost and benefit analysis and return on investment calculations. Not only is this key for programme approval and prioritisation, it should serve as a reference throughout the programme as to why you are spending all that time and money.

> *"Everyone on the programme should be engaged with the vision and slaves to the business case"*
>
> *testing manager*

Many programme managers confess that the business case is put on the shelf until the end of the programme. It is often not until post implementation that the strategy, overall objectives and benefits are reviewed. This is obviously too late to make corrections to the requirements or design. At every stage in the programme the key deliverables need to be tested against the business case. This is the most critical document for those managers measured on delivery costs, schedule, and the realisation of benefits.

However, for the hundreds of people engaged in the programme and the thousands impacted by it, the business case is just a complex and meaningless document written in a foreign language. There needs to be something simpler and more meaningful to everyone. A vision will have been clearly stated in terms of business strategy and enabling the future business goals. But again, this is not easily accessible or understood by everyone because it often uses a language that is not relevant to them. Therefore, we need something different, something simple but powerful that encapsulates the end state of the programme.

We need something that can be understood and felt by everyone, something personal to the masses.

> *"I thought, 'who on earth has a personal vision statement?' And then I got one and I now know where I'm going and why"*
>
> *operations manager*

There are a number of questions a programme vision must try and answer, all built around a "what's in it for me/us?" theme:

- How will life be different?
- What will it look and feel like?
- Why should I want this programme to be a success?
- Why do I want to be a part of it?

The 'me/us' part of the question could be an individual or a group of individuals in a small team or large division. The vision can be a single statement, a picture, an icon, or a few key words. The important factor is that it is instantly recognisable, memorable and relevant to its audience.

The programme is going to have a life of its own and therefore needs an identity, a brand. Use of professional marketing people will help bring the programme alive and provide a purpose and sense of belonging for everyone touched by the programme throughout its life.

In naming the programme and providing the vision, avoid the use of targets or words that may change or be outside of your control e.g. dates, financial targets, and locations. I remember a programme called 'Project 90', named by its target completion date. It fell into disrepute through missing the year because of legitimate reasons and was difficult to re-invigorate. It ultimately completed in 1993 and was incorrectly branded as a failure by some outsiders.

It is inevitable that over a long period of time that the programme will evolve in some of its tangible shape. However, if the vision or purpose changes then it is a different programme and would need stopping and re-launching.

> *"Success means survival and bonuses, failure means the death of this business... is that clear enough?"*
>
> *programme sponsor*

The vision statement in quotes above is clearly signalling the reason for change - survival. It was in response to a question asking for an explanation as to why a big and disruptive programme needed to be done now. It clearly answers the question of why it's needed and also has a carrot in the bonuses, albeit in a more threatening manner than I would like. But it is only a platform for further detailed statements for each impacted area to answer what it means to them. It is an overarching statement that will be brought to life by speeches, workshops, documents, film, pictures and any other possible creative methods. The vision is about hearts and minds and it is this that makes for successful programmes delivering sustainable change.

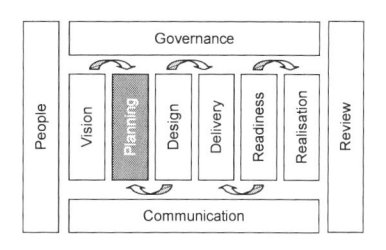

2

Planning

Preparation is everything

Topics include:
- Resource planning
- Stakeholder expectations
- Assessing capability
- Supplier selection
- Supplier management
- Planning the exit

2: Planning
Preparation is everything

Am I the only one who knows I'm right?
by a programme manager

[In the middle of the build phase the programme manager was asked to step down from the role and ultimately left the organisation. To protect the person's identity some of the more trivial content has been altered].

As a senior manager in the company I was asked to manage our largest ever systems programme. Having had a successful career in finance and operations I was ideally placed to drive the transition to new systems and migrate from our 30-year old legacy systems. The business case was financially strong but more importantly the new system would enable new areas of business that our current systems couldn't support. The executive team had already chosen the solution and supplier so my job was to manage the enhancements with the supplier and the migration with the in-house team.

The planning process was fairly straightforward. I got quotes from the supplier and from the in-house IT architecture team. I added 20% contingency because, well, you know what IT estimates are like. The total elapsed time was 1 year, which was fine because that gave me 4 months contingency before we had to deliver the changes for a regulatory deadline.

At first I had a great relationship with the supplier and we went on quite a few hospitality events together. I became friends with their directors and they were very responsive to any additional changes we needed. It was the in-house IT department that were more of a problem. They clearly didn't support the migration and were always being so negative with their comments and worse, their increasing estimates. I knew they were putting up artificial barriers and so pretty much ignored their whining. The scope of the programme was increasing as we were identifying more benefit from the new functions. We also decided to upgrade to the suppliers new version of their software, which was well advanced in its development. I thought that should have kept the IT people quiet, as it was all the latest gizmos. But no, they just continued to raise risks rather than adopt the 'can do' attitude of the supplier.

The first problem I had with the supplier was when they showed me their latest plan. The date had pushed out 3 months because of the additional scope and the costs had risen accordingly. This meant my plan was no longer valid and I knew the board would have an issue with it so I pushed back and said I wanted them to deliver on time but would accept the cost increase as we were getting additional benefit. The board accepted this as the ROI actually increased and we still had the 4 months contingency. The supplier added contractors and was working a 7-day week, with overtime, to get the delivery back on schedule. The in-house IT plan remained the same.

The supplier then announced at the next progress meeting that costs had escalated because of contractors and overtime and they couldn't get back all the time lost. We would have to incur the 3-month delay or reduce the scope. After a few more meetings I decided to keep the pressure on the build stage and change the plan to overlap some testing phases. This gained us a month but still had some slippage. The next board meeting was particularly uncomfortable but I focussed on the additional benefit, the 2-month contingency we still had, and fact that big change programmes often hit problems but we would manage our way through it. The internal IT guys were not supporting the new plan but they never really did anyway.

The IT team now told me that the migration could not be done in time for the regulatory deadline because they weren't receiving the code for the new system in time. They proposed diverting resource to do the regulatory changes on the legacy system to ensure we were compliant by the required date. This was just another way of them trying to hang on to their old systems and scupper the plan. I insisted they did overtime and worked weekends like the supplier. They demanded the same pay and we compromised.

The board got nervous and decided to have an external audit of the programme. Of course they were paid to find problems and so they did. I was removed from the programme having committed blood sweat and tears to it for months. It even affected my home life and for that I was rewarded with being a scapegoat. I was stitched up by the IT department, the supplier, and the external auditor. The programme delivered late, over budget with reduced scope and the migration didn't happen. They decided against the product as a strategic solution and forever more the programme was referred to as a joke and an example of how not to run a programme.

With just this short story it doesn't take much analysis to figure out all the mistakes, and so many of them were in the planning stage or in the need for ongoing planning throughout the programme. If I were to take a hard view then I would say it was an individual who wouldn't listen and got what he deserved. A more sympathetic view is that he was out of his depth and it was the person who assigned him to the programme who should have taken some of the heat. He was unsupported and afraid of failure and didn't recognise his own shortcomings. Here's a brief assessment of the issues:

- Insufficient experience for a major programme
- Skimping on the initial planning detail
- Not involving all the contributors to the programme
- Ignoring warnings he didn't want to hear
- Scope creep
- Not re-planning whenever significant change occurred
- Not doing regular risk analysis
- Time and materials contract
- New software platform
- Inclusion of time-critical regulatory change
- Covering up issues from board reporting
- Putting early reliance on overtime
- Planning phase overlaps
- Insufficient contingency

If that appears all rather negative then yes it probably is, but learning from mistakes and failure is often the easiest way to improve performance. The corresponding best practice statements are easily determined.

Lets now look at some of the high impact and consistently reported issues with the planning stage of a change programme.

Support for the plan

We've already established that one of the critical success factors for a change programme is gaining the hearts and minds of everyone involved. We've discussed this from a vision point of view but how do we do this for the plan? Plans are always wrong at the outset, so why bother? That attitude is why so many programmes don't do enough planning and don't do it well. And that's why so many programmes go way over budget and way beyond the planned end date.

The link between vision and planning is the business case and this is one of the most important documents throughout the programme. It should be a living document that is understood by everyone, which means having different versions for different audiences. Each version would state the objectives and outcomes in a way that is relevant to them. It is a great advantage to have everyone involved in delivering the programme to understand what needs to be done, by when, but also why. What are the benefits, the outcomes and the impacts? Face to face briefings with plenty of opportunity for Q&A will engage people at the start, increasing motivation and buy-in. All subsequent planning documents should be able to link back to the business case; project plans, benefit realisation plans, resource plans, organisation plans.

> *"Just deliver the plan, they said. But it was the first time I'd seen it and the plan was horribly wrong"*
>
> *IT project manager*

High level planning and estimation is an art as much as a science. Yes, there are many tools and databases to help and should be used. But the most powerful and accurate estimating tool is often the experience and intuition of the people who have done it many times before. I always use these people to give me an initial view of the plan and then ask them to sense check the data from the scientific approach, frequently applying an adjustment - the experience factor.

It is worth involving external help in producing the first plan that you'll commit to. If you are getting external help in delivery then they should be bought into the plans so that the contract can include an element of fixed price or risk & reward. As many different eyes as possible should challenge and evolve the initial plan.

It has been confirmed by many people in this research that only by involving every person and group of people that will be either delivering or impacted by the programme will you get full support. It should be very clear that the plan will change as the programme evolves through the life cycle and therefore it is essential to keep that involvement at each stage. This will keep the support of the teams throughout the programme and retain their hearts and minds. Transparent and honest communication of progress and decisions will also keep the group ownership of the plan.

Resource Planning

We've discussed the importance of involving everyone in the planning stage, but how do we determine who is going to be involved? Planning how to source each stage of the programme should be done early as it will be more difficult to win the support of people who join the party late and it will require more changes to the plan every time a new party has input. A simple method of determining the types of resource you need is by using a competency matrix such as the one below.

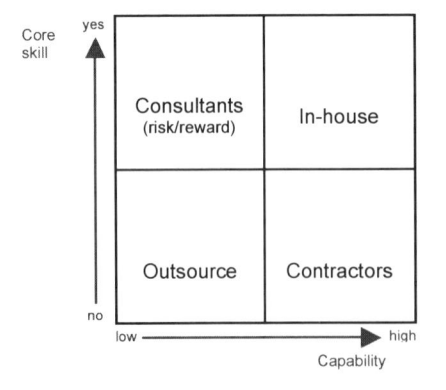

Core skill	yes		
		Consultants (risk/reward)	In-house
		Outsource	Contractors
	no		
		low —————————► high
		Capability	

The diagram shows a model competency matrix.

Outsourcing of low value skills or non-core activity, or use of contractors depends on how much internal capability is in place. For high value skills without competence, the use of consultants on site provides more delivery certainty (a higher cost option but critical to success).

Dependencies on learning critical skills in order to deliver a programme should be avoided by using proven external experience to compliment internal capability. However, learning must be incorporated into the plan if there is a need to increase in-house capability in order to be more self-sufficient in future programmes. This is not needed if the programme is likely to be a one-off event, such as a platform migration.

A couple of consistent themes coming from the experience from the research regarding support for the plan were:

- Estimation should be top down initially and then bottom up for full buy-in from all parties.
- Quotes from suppliers should be fixed where possible and risk/reward introduced for big contracts. This ensures everyone has 'skin in the game'

Stakeholder expectations

The initial plan is the contract with your stakeholders. You can tell them that the plan is going to change as we learn more, and as external factors change, but they will still use the first plan to judge ultimate delivery success or failure. So it's worth putting in the effort and getting it as close to reality as you can. The chart below, based on real data, may help manage the stakeholders' expectations for changes to the plan (but I doubt it).

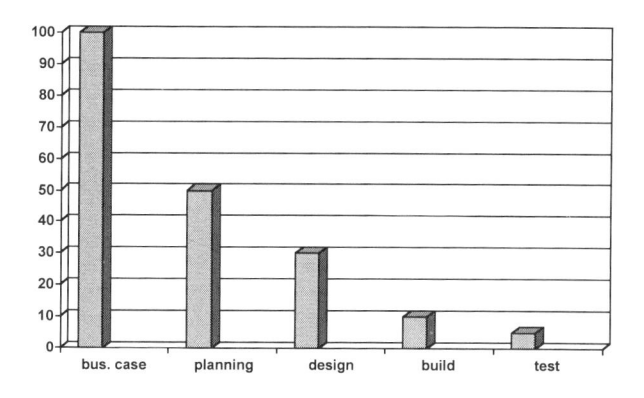

The chart shows the percentage accuracy of a total programme cost estimate at the end of each stage. The number that stakeholders really struggle with is that after writing a business case, the cost may vary by plus or minus 50% (and as we all know, programme costs rarely go down). The data is based on real experience but I think that if the planning stage is done well then a target percentage variance should be more like 20 than 50. This brings us to two more themes from the experience data:

- Plan for significant cost variances in the business case and make sure the worst case still stacks up.
- Use real data experiences to support the need for variances and then target an improvement against those.

Can we do this alone?

We've spent the last umpteen years being good at what we are good at. It should come as no surprise to anyone that when we try and make changes, it can be extremely challenging. So we need help, but from whom, for what, and when?

Help for a specific programme is ok but most organisations are seeking an ongoing capability and have ambitions to become an agile organisation that is responsive to internal and external demands for change. So we should work out what aspects of change we want as core capability and what areas we either need temporary help with or permanent outsourcing. A previous competency matrix showed us how to select resource solutions based on capability. But how do we assess our own capability.

The change capability cycle diagram below is a good place to start. You will be able to recognise where you are through simple statements. Wherever your start point is, you should take one step at a time in progressing to the more advanced stages. Depending on your business strategy it may be that you don't wish to go to stage 4 and be a centre of excellence for change (although unlikely if you are reading this book). Whatever level you are at it is likely that you will need some external help and, particularly at level 4, this is not a sign of weakness but a conscious strategy. There is no shame in getting help where you are less experienced or have no need to develop skills in an area of non-competitive advantage.

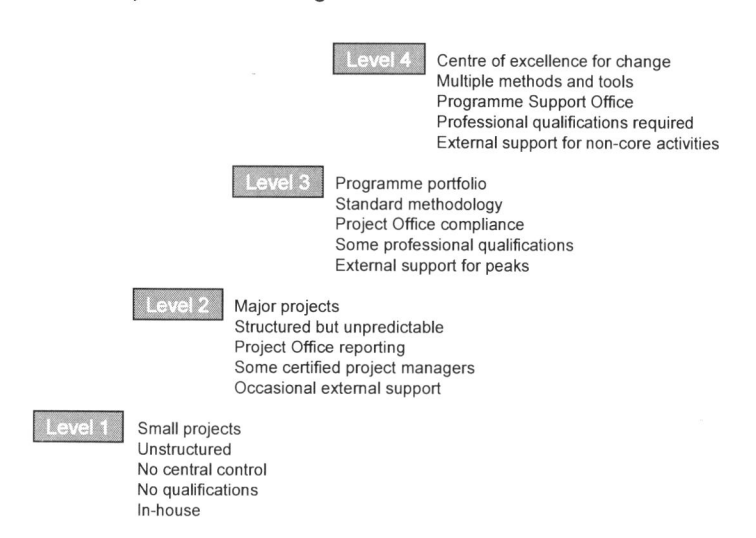

Level 4
Centre of excellence for change
Multiple methods and tools
Programme Support Office
Professional qualifications required
External support for non-core activities

Level 3
Programme portfolio
Standard methodology
Project Office compliance
Some professional qualifications
External support for peaks

Level 2
Major projects
Structured but unpredictable
Project Office reporting
Some certified project managers
Occasional external support

Level 1
Small projects
Unstructured
No central control
No qualifications
In-house

The next few pages focus on the experiences and best practice associated with external programme support; who to use, what to use them for, when to use them, how to manage them, and importantly, when to let them go.

Suppliers – partners or pests?

The answer to this question much depends on whom you're asking. A programme manager or sponsor will likely see a high performing supplier as an integral player in the programme and critical for success. However, if you ask some of the in-house team they will often refer to them as unwelcome aliens who have different motives, different methods, and no care for the long-term future of the business or its people. Both views can be right. There are a number of critical factors in using suppliers of programme services:

- Select the right cultural fit
- Find the right skills for the right job

- Choose the right type of contract
- Align the goals, acknowledge the differences
- Openly brief the reasons for using them
- Plan entry and exit criteria

Supplier Selection

The first two bullets above, on supplier selection, can be dealt with together. The usual RFI (request for information) tender document should be used along with interviews, presentations and whatever good procurement practice is in place in the organisation. The supplier selection model below is an example of a simple way of recording the organisations experiences of different services throughout the lifecycle (the names and ratings are purely illustrative and do not reflect my judgement of capability).

Strategic Thinking	Strategic Planning	Project Planning	Project Delivery	Ernst & Young	Accenture	Cap Gemini	CSC	IBM
McKinsey	Ernst & Young	Ernst & Young	Project Mgmt	1	1	1	1	1
Booz Allen	Accenture	Accenture	Project Office	1	1	1	1	1
McKinsey	PA	PA	Health Check	1	1	1	1	1
	IBM	IBM	Systems	0	1	1	1	1
		CSC	Process	0	1	2	2	1
			People	0	2	2	2	2

0 = service not offered
1 = specialisation
2 = experienced

This model can be used to help create a shortlist that is relevant to the assignment and to your organisation. It is important to keep the model up to date as the consultancy world is forever changing, and is another reason why the diagram is only an example to be used as a framework for your own ratings from your own experience. For example, the Cap Gemini and Ernst & Young merger and then de-merger in the early 2000s may have caused confusion of what services were provided from which group and also a change to the cultures of each organisation.

In addition to a high-level selection model, it is useful to keep a database of supplier experiences with some simple rating for a number of key performance indicators. This may include the following:

- Meeting contractual agreement
- Additional value provided
- Cultural fit
- Keeping promises
- Integrating with process and methods
- Conflict resolution
- Quality of resource
- Handover
- Coaching/mentoring

A simple scoring of 1-5 for each category will create a supplier rating that will be a useful guide as experience is accumulated over many change programmes. The rating shouldn't be used for final decision making or replacing existing selection methods but can help produce a good shortlist and prevent a lot of wasted time during the selection process.

"I spent too long reviewing literature and meeting salesmen. A trusted supplier evaluation database would have saved me loads of time"

strategy analyst

If kept simple, experience databases are quick and easy and capture useful information that can no longer be extracted from people once they have moved on or have forgotten.

The culture and the key individuals often get overlooked at the selection stage but can make the difference between good and bad relationships throughout the programme. But how do you determine the culture of the organisation and how do you ensure they will continually provide high quality people? We have all seen the A-team arrive in pre-sales stage and then gradually be replaced by more junior resource.

The experience database should provide some insight to these issues but in the event that a mature database is not available we have to use interview techniques and references. In interviews and reference calls/visits there is usually a strong focus on the deliverables and costs. In order to not dilute this focus there should be a person whose role is to determine cultural fit. They should be skilled and experienced in these kinds of interviews and should be given equal time and access to the right people.

"The consultants were just higher paid versions of us, but without the knowledge. Their additional skill was sucking up to the management, with a posh accent"

in-house developer

The senior players in a supplier are key to negotiating the deal and resolving conflicts throughout the programme. But they will not be doing all the work and so it is important to meet as many of the key people who will be assigned to the programme as possible. There should be agreements of duration on the programme with exit criteria for all key individuals. There should also be an agreement that people can be exchanged on the programme at the request of the customer. This of course all changes if there is an outsourced type contract.

Choosing the contract

It has been stated a few times in this document that a 'risk & reward' contract is preferable in a change programme. This is the experience of most contributors to this book, however it is not always appropriate. The benefits of a risk & reward type of contract are:

- Certainty of cost (remember to budget for over-delivery bonuses)
- High likelihood of delivery or over-delivery to schedule
- Transparency of reward, leading to trust

The risks associated with a risk/reward contract are:

- Scope is ill-defined or not managed tightly
- Total focus on hard deliverables and neglect of softer, less defined deliverables
- Goals are not aligned

Managing the risks is key to a successful risk/reward contract. If the scope can be well defined prior to pricing and scheduling then a good change control process can manage the changes. If softer deliverables are important, such as handover to trained colleagues of the customer, then these need to be defined and weighted in the contract i.e. a percentage of payment attributed to softer deliverables. If a significant element of the deliverables cannot be undisputedly defined then a time and materials contract may be more appropriate.

Align the goals, acknowledge the differences

One of the biggest challenges of a contract with a delivery partner, whether they are a systems integrator or cultural change supplier, is the alignment of goals. An 'us and them' relationship can quickly build and there is a huge risk to delivery if there is distrust. The natural scepticism of the customer's colleagues is to assume they are being rewarded differently, and a lot higher.

The key lesson from the experiences in this area was to make the goals as transparent as possible. There will always be differences so let's acknowledge them, bring them out in the open, and work out ways of dealing with them.

> *"I never trusted the suppliers team until I saw the contract, then I actually had some sympathy for them"*
>
> *project manager*

An example from one project is when the relationship between teams was breaking down to a very destructive level because of the perception of pay reward differences. The supplier team were working longer days and believed to be paid overtime. This gave the impression of trying to shame the customer's teams whilst being paid for every hour. When it was made known that the supplier team were actually paid a salary without overtime plus a bonus for delivering to schedule, there was more empathy for the long hours. This also resulted in an opportunity for the customer's teams to forfeit their overtime payments for a similar bonus structure. The rewards were the same and the delivery goal, to achieve a bonus, was aligned. The team united, the relationships formed, and the combined goals were met.

As much as this was a good intervention, the goals should have been aligned at the outset and baked in the contract for everyone to see.

An example of a less tangible goal is to increase the capability of the customer's teams such that they are self-sufficient once 'the experts' have moved on. It's easy to measure the tangible elements of training, documentation, new tools and processes.

But the measurement of capability is more subjective and its success is often only evident when the suppliers have long gone. Most experiences of such a goal in a contract are that it is always lowest priority and often conflicts with delivery. Because it is less measurable it is usually agreed as a met goal because it can't be proved either way.

A goal that is difficult to measure or evidence its success shouldn't be in the contract as a risk & reward element. A time and materials basis, with a good cost/time estimate, will ensure the job is done and that the relationship is not strained by a dispute.

If you need to refer to the contract, the relationship is dead

The heading above is an often-quoted expression, which in sentiment is supported by experience. It refers to the need to use the contract when there is a dispute over a deliverable, payment, scope definition, or other tangible measure of success. It is true that in most cases if the dispute cannot be managed through escalation and a compromise agreed then the relationship will be at breaking point.

The most important relationship between supplier and customer is at the top. The account director and programme director (or similar roles) must display positive behaviours speaking with one voice about aligned goals. They must manage disputes with one voice, show compromise and support each other to both sets of teams.

One experience that demonstrated the value of a strong director level relationship was during a dispute over a change control and who was going to pay.

The issue was escalated by project managers and cost accountants in the project office. The dispute had split the teams and the relationship was deteriorating. The escalation to the directors was via a project meeting with a large attendance. The two versions of the cost were presented along with the justifications for a high and low number. It was not clear whether the change control should have been in original scope or not so the directors agreed, in one sentence, to split the cost. They followed up with a joint lecture on the wasted time and money spent on the dispute and how detrimental it was to the aligned goals.

The teams went away somewhat embarrassed having expected a small war to erupt. The directors left as they arrived, a single voice. They then went into an office and argued the point for half an hour with some ferocity, but no-one saw it. The team were left in no doubt that there would be no division at the top and that escalation was seen as failure. The directors continued to battle in private but always came to a decision that was supported by both of them. They also went on to deliver more programmes for the organisation and became a formidable partnership with a loyal following on both sides.

"We didn't always agree, and fell out badly a few times. But we didn't let anyone see and always spoke with one voice to both teams"

programme director

Here's a quick example of where the director relationship can go very wrong. One project, with heavy supplier reliance, was headed by two directors with very large egos. When the first dispute (over a design detail which was more religious than scientific) arose, neither party would back down or compromise. They also aligned their teams behind their view and caused a division throughout the programme. Ultimately, the supplier was dismissed and legal proceedings were undertaken. This risk would never be in a contract but the relationship at the top is as important as the contract itself. The learning here was that the directors had different beliefs about IT architecture and it is imperative that these opinions are understood at the outset, during facilitated discovery workshops or, perhaps more productively, over dinner.

> *"It was all out war. Everyone forgot what the goals were and focussed on how to win battles. God knows how much money it cost us and them"*
>
> IT architect

There are times when reference to the contract can be of benefit. If the contract terms are made visible to everyone (preferably not in the legal speak which most contracts are written in) then it can be a good communication vehicle. Similar to the re-iteration of the vision throughout the programme, it can serve as a useful reminder for the aligned goals, the agreed scope, or measurement of success or exit criteria. This continual sharing of goals will ensure everyone is focussed on the right things as one team. An alternative to the contract, mainly because of language (plus some elements are likely to be confidential), is a programme charter. This can simplify the goals and also be used to add in some softer requirements such as behaviours. However, if the charter isn't directly aligned to the rewards then it will be ignored. Aligning rewards and goals is essential for buy-in to a charter.

Planning for transition to BAU

In a programme with a heavy use of external resource it is important to plan for the transition of tasks and skills to the in-house team. Although this is an obvious statement to make, there is a trend in the book's research that tells us this is often overlooked in favour of a focus on delivery. Many internal teams felt dumped on without a controlled transition and felt unable to fulfil the roles they were asked to do, either in completing the programme or in a support and maintenance role.

The resource transition plan is another document that should be made public so that there is total transparency of when handover is planned to take place. It can then be the co-ownership of all parties to ensure that this happens, with escalation if it doesn't.

> *"I was left high and dry with a new system to support and no more than a 10 minute handover. No-one ever had the time for me"*
>
> *support analyst*

The implications of not delivering on the resource transition plan are:
- Increase in cost of external resource who have to stay on beyond the plan.
- Late programme delivery due to the inability of internal resources to fulfil project roles.
- Customer service degradation through the inability to support new systems and processes.

The resource plan graph below-left is taken from a programme where the transition was part of the exit criteria for the supplier.

The top line is the supplier resource who were leading the programme and providing most of the resource. The bottom line is the internal resource plan. There is a clear point at which the handover plan must have been achieved in order for the internal team to complete and support the change.

The second graph to the right shows the actual resource deployment. There are two significant differences. Firstly, early in the programme the internal resource was late in being fully allocated to the programme. In order to keep to the schedule the supplier resource was increased. This had no detrimental impact on the delivery (or transition plan) but increased cost. The second difference is the additional resource allocated by the supplier in order to complete to schedule. This was the right thing to do in a time-boxed programme and the programme contingency met the additional cost. However, there was no corresponding extension for either resource to affect the handover plan and therefore the transition occurred without handover. The impact to the programme was not apparent until the warranty period when the fixes to systems and processes were delivered to poor quality due to the lack of knowledge and skills of the internal resources. The programme advocacy was poor and the sustainability of the change was in question. The supplier was brought back in to remedy the situation and implement the handover as well as the warranty changes. Imagine how the internal resource team felt?

3

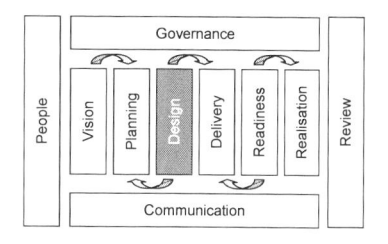

Design
Rubbish in, rubbish out

Topics include:
    Scope management
    Architecture
    Design authority
    Requirements
    Innovation versus proven
    Simple solutions

3: Design
Rubbish in, rubbish out

Design can be the difference between success and failure of a programme and also can be the greatest source of competitive advantage.

Good design gives you a better chance of delivery success and bad design will result in cost and time overrun. Bad design will also decrease your chances of realising the all-important benefits. These are obvious statements but ones that need continual focus throughout the programme, not just in the early stages. In fact, in this research there are more examples of failure caused by poor design than any other factor in a programme.

An old dog learns a new trick
by a business analyst.

Why do the big changes always get sprung on you? One minute I was working in the office, 15 minutes from home, doing a role I was comfortable with and I saw very little need for change. The next minute, in fact the next Monday morning, I was working in an office 100 miles from home, staying in a hotel and doing something I'd never heard of before, let alone have any skills in. But despite the poor handling of the changes from a management point of view, this turned out to be the best thing that ever happened to me.

I wouldn't say I was a plodder, but I was certainly a thorough and reliable analyst. I knew how to gather requirements, document them, facilitate walkthroughs, and translate business speak into functional and technical specifications. My document management was legendary and I was responsible for bringing in a brilliant new automated version control system. I liked my routine and my comforts. I had a desk with my family photos on it, a regular seat in the canteen with the same crowd, and enough time in the evenings to feed my passion for cycling. I was known for my knowledge and respected for my quality of work. Then the new guy came in with his fancy ideas.

We were in the planning stage of a new major programme with some pretty aggressive dates on it to deliver a re-launch of a new product range. External promises had already been made (the sales people always sold what we didn't have in order to get things developed quickly) and so the date was the critical factor. Budget was also fixed, so it was only scope that was a variable. This was going to need some real discipline over requirements definition, documentation sign-off, and scope management. That is, if there was going to be any documentation!

I was fully aware of all the new fads for systems design and each year there seemed to be a new buzz word from consultants trying to sell the same re-packaged ideas: rapid application development, accelerated development centres, joint application design, rapid design workshops, to name a few. We had used some prototyping before, to good effect, and we had always used walkthroughs for change management and developing pre-signoff documentation. Our user engagement was good and we had developed some real experts with knowledge of their specific systems and processes. When we got these people on the team we were pretty certain of success. But what we were about to go through wasn't a step further but a major leap into the unknown.

We arrived on the Monday morning and no sooner had we hung our coats up, we were sitting on coloured bean bags in a big room that looked and felt more like a children's nursery than a work place. In spite of my apprehension I did join in with a game that solved a huge wooden puzzle. The other guinea pigs for this were a few people from my analyst team, some developers, testers, a couple of trainers, and whole host of business users. There were also a lot of people I didn't recognise and it turned out they were from the consultancy. After a very good breakfast buffet, which I ate too much of, we were told that there would be no training or lectures about this new approach to systems design, we would be joining some established teams and be working straight away. Now I was really panicking. How do they expect me to learn quickly enough without even an overview, let alone technical skills training on the new tool-set.

Our new project had already been split into modules and the teams allocated to designing a number of modules each. My team was 6 people, including a module leader (consultant) and 3 business users, which just left a consultant and me. Our first module was to design the new process flow and screens for a customer to get a quote for the new product range. This included a complex decision tree. We were in a 'pod', which had a round table that doubled as a white board, and was in an enclosed space made up of 7-foot white board walls. There was one PC with a very large screen. Where were the chairs?

The module leader started to draw the process flow on the wall. We all chipped in and agreed it was 80% right. We made a list of questions we couldn't answer on one of the walls. This was because we didn't have all the right people in the pod with the right knowledge. The leader then said we had done enough for now and were going to present it to the wider group. I was horrified by this because it was a scruffy diagram on a wall and was not complete. We were going to be hugely embarrassed.

We had a break for snacks and drinks and 10 minutes later the room was made up of lots of walls turned round to the middle of the room with us standing in the centre. In turn, each leader presented their first stage design to the wider group, which had *all the knowledge we needed. They facilitated a quick feedback session and got answers to the questions. The other consultant was making the changes to the process flow on the fly. After a few minutes the whole room was happy with the diagram. This was repeated for all the other modules and teams and, after a session to ensure the modules were all joined up, we returned to our pod. Having got a process flow it was now onto screen design. As now expected, this was done quickly, on the PC with the big screen, by the consultant. We all chipped in on what fields should be on what screen based on the process flow. The validation and rules were done straight on the prototype. Again, there were unanswered questions and dependencies on other modules. This time I was more comfortable as I knew how they would be answered. In the next group session we saw how the design was building, without requirements! I was beginning to understand the process here – 80% solutions very quickly and then wider input following an iterative approach. I wasn't sure when we would stop iterating and who's job it was going to be to document all this and get it signed off by management once they'd made their changes. I discovered there was going to be no management intervention and no documentation to sign off!*

The people were fully empowered to design the system and the prototype was the documentation for the real IT build to work from. The walls were regularly photographed before being erased so we had a record of every version and every question and answer. As far as iterations were concerned, the modules were handed out as daily tasks so we would do as many as required before we went home (or to the hotel). On later reflection I realised that this time boxing approach was excellent for when budget and time were fixed and scope was the only variable. At the time I just felt exhausted, but satisfied with our days work. I was still very concerned for the quality.

The day was long but went so quickly. We had achieved more in a day than we usually would in a week. The consultants joined us for dinner at the hotel and again we sat with our teams. We reflected on the day and discussed the pros and cons of the methodology, the emotional roller coaster, the 'on the job' training and the lack of documentation! On my way to bed the leader gave me a text book and asked me to read the first 4 chapters if I was interested in what I had learned today. I fell asleep mid chapter 2.

The week ended Friday at 3.30pm. I drove home exhausted and exhilarated. We had just designed a major part of a new system in a week. We got all the knowledge we needed, we got sign-off from the business users, and we learned some new techniques and the beginning of a whole new methodology. I'd had quite a few heated debates and challenges about the approach. I had many 'arms folded' moments and fell out with a few people. It was emotional in many ways and I'm not known for expressing my emotions. One person hated it so much they went off sick the following week and were taken off the project. I felt sorry for her as personal circumstances made it really difficult for such significant and unplanned change.

At the end of the design phase of the programme I had made the tough journey from sceptic to advocate. I was given the unofficial title of method champion and was to lead the next programme's design phase. Unfortunately, once the consultants had left, the facilities and tools left with them. We didn't invest in what was required for the future and so we returned to the old ways. I joined the consultancy soon after receiving my annual bonus.

The story is common among many analysts going through changing methods and tools. This analyst coped really well and went through a significant transition through being thrown in at the deep end. Here are some good and bad practices extracted from the analyst's experience.

Good practice

- A 'deep end' approach works for those who adapt well to change.
- On-the-job learning is supported by theoretical learning.
- Planning of the design phase in structured time-boxed modules.
- Joint design with customers, acting as one team with shared goals.
- Extensive use of prototyping and (limited) automated documentation.
- Small teams with 80% solutions followed by wider input to complete the task.
- Creative, productive environments with tools and facilities.

Bad practice

- Poor management of expectations of change.
- No recognition of individuals' current value before they change roles.
- 'Deep end' doesn't work for those who don't adapt well to change.
- Wasted learning through not investing in tools and methods.
- Selling the outcome externally before planning the change required.
- A disregard for individual personal circumstances.

The book's research highlighted seven key areas of experience during the design stage of a programme: Scope, Architecture, Governance, Requirements, Innovation, Simplicity, and *Pareto*.

Scope management

The management of scope is almost always raised as a key reason for overrun. It is a constant battle to resist scope increases and very hard to say no when it all appears justifiable.

Here are some helpful tips from experience of doing this well and not so well:

- Keep scope focussed on the programme objectives; don't try and solve all of the company's problems in one programme. Re-iterate the programme vision and objectives, then regularly review scope against these and be disciplined to say no.
- Keep a track of change controls, those accepted and rejected. The agreed scope changes list is essential to keep stakeholders supporting the programme and not throwing bricks at the non-delivery of promised function. If business stakeholders respond to scope changes with "that means I can no longer deliver my business plan" then you have lost their support and they will disassociate themselves with the programme or even worse become saboteurs.
- Always look for opportunities to reduce and simplify. It's not one person's job, it's a mind-set for everyone. Again, reference to the outcomes and benefits should focus the mind and prevent over complex 'nice to have' changes. Quantity of change is not the end goal, it's delivering the benefits, short and long term.
- The sponsor's role is critical in scope management and they will need reminding of that, and advising of the appropriate decisions to make. Don't be afraid to escalate and use their authority, particularly when dealing with senior business stakeholders who are struggling to accept scope reduction.
- Every piece of additional scope should have a corresponding benefit that can be measured in isolation. Future enablers are worthy but should be in a next phase and justified against other priorities. The addition of justified scope is the biggest risk to overrun unless a corresponding amount of scope is removed.
- Use statistics and case studies to remind people of the negative impact of scope creep. Make these threats as close to home as possible. Most companies should have examples

of where it went wrong before and this is the most powerful information to persuade people to resist scope creep.

For an illustration of how damaging scope creep can be I can refer to a project in a financial services organisation where an implementation date had been communicated externally. This wasn't necessarily the smartest thing to do at the outset as the pressure was immediately on the team to deliver to a date based on early estimates. Therefore tight control of the scope was essential and estimates rarely go down, it was likely that scope needed to be reduced or solutions simplified as the project progressed.

Predictably, dates came under pressure in the plan during design. This was the time to reduce scope and simplify the programme, maybe even delaying non-essential projects. However, the programme director decided to allow for improvements following pressure from business stakeholders. The web project was now massive and required additional people. The solution was exciting for the business and had real benefit and potential for competitive advantage. The programme director was temporarily a hero as he presented this to the board. But he was blind to the impact on the date.

"We all knew we were in trouble, but every time the programme director had bad news to tell the board, he just promised more scope"

project manager

Inevitably, there were some tough choices to be made. They could either delay and embarrass the company externally, or phase projects and embarrass the programme team, or take a risk on quality. Again, not wishing to give bad news and not listening to the programme team, the programme director decided to avoid the scope management decision and took a risk.

A few weeks before implementation the programme team escalated over the top of the programme director and the quality issues were made known. A rescue team were sent in and they had to delay the programme (external embarrassment), phase the projects over several months (internal embarrassment) and accept a major cost and time overrun. The scope management was ultimately faced up to but done so late that the programme was a big failure. The original scope didn't ever get implemented and the technical solution changed under new programme management.

This is a very similar to the story in the planning chapter of this book but is a different programme in a different company. The frequent occurrence of scope creep causing programme delivery failure makes it worth repeating.

Architecture

The definition and delivery of architecture is key to sustainable change. As well as a blueprint for delivering the programme, the benefits of the architectures are often post implementation and sometimes forgotten or considered lower priority. Architectures are essential to the delivery of the operating model and ongoing benefits. They can protect the future flexibility, lower costs, and increase speed to market; all areas that, if delivered well, can provide ongoing competitive advantage.

Design is often seen as a stage in the programme, as I have depicted it in this book. Where this is true for a phase in a methodology, it is not true in regard to the philosophy or principles described in this chapter. Design principles are relevant throughout the cycle. The same applies to architecture. Many people focus on systems architecture in a programme and then have various other diagrams, models, or maps for defining the blueprint for other parts of the business such as people, strategy, and processes. These should also be considered part of the programme architecture because they all need to be connected. An integrated architecture covering all areas of the business is important for achieving true transformation of a business.

Stage	Architecture
Vision	Business model
	Policy model
	Business plan
Planning	Business case
	Programme plan
Design	Business process model
	Data model
	Application architecture
	Technology architecture
Delivery	Development methodology
Readiness	Test strategy
	Test environment architecture
Realisation	Benefit realisation plan
Governance	Controls
	Reporting model
People	Organisation model
	Resource strategy and plan
	Values
Communication	Communications plan
	Programme charter
	Stakeholder map
Review	Review model
	Learning database

The table above shows some of the key elements of an integrated architecture for a programme. It is only an example because there may be more or less models and blueprints required depending on the breadth of change. It's also not for the purists as I realise this doesn't conform to a traditional enterprise framework. The main purpose is to remind you that there are models, rules, plans and policies for each area and stage of change and they should be linked into one guide for everyone to follow.

Governance

The role of a design authority is critical. This group of experts are the custodians of the business architecture and the IT architecture. In a methodology a process needs to be in place to ensure all design documents help deliver the target architectures. But before that the programme team need educating in the target architectures throughout the programme. Similar to the vision, this is not a one off exercise that is briefed and then put on the shelf. Consider building a house and all agreeing the architects' drawings at the outset, then the builders never refer to the plans. The likelihood is they would build a sound house that on the surface meets the needs of the owner. But after moving in, the owner would find some detail that was missing or some inflexibility over future modifications.

Some useful experiences relating to architecture are:

- Business processes, systems, customer outputs, and organisation should all be designed as one integrated solution.
- Stick to some clear principles but allow for flexibility, as things will change as you learn more.
- Test the design early, prototype and pilot where possible. It'll cost a lot more to change later in the development cycle. Also, early deliverables are a good motivator.
- Performance and security are often forgotten areas that cause major problems later on – ensure these are clearly defined in the target architecture and tested as early as possible.

- Ensure the cost of ongoing support and change to the design is known and is in the business case.

Our Requirements

"They don't listen or understand us"
"They don't tell us what we need to know"
"They speak a different language"
"They don't know what they want"

How many times have you heard these kinds of divisive comments from programme people and their customers around a lack of understanding?

Here are some ways of reducing the risk of misunderstanding and miscommunication, which inevitably adds cost and time and produces the wrong solutions.

- Focus the requirements on business needs that satisfy the business case and that will deliver the benefits. Don't write a long document full of desired outcomes and don't attempt to design technical solutions at this stage. Many analysts describe this as their biggest de-motivation; being given solutions and not problems. The designers are the experts and need to work from a problem, not an instruction.
- Use professional business analysts to write requirements. It is more important to have skilled and experienced people who can define requirements than those with business knowledge and who are easily made available but don't have the skills.
- Real discipline is required over signed off requirements prior to development (if you're using a waterfall method).
- Don't try and replicate the same processes and solutions in a new system. Focus on the real needs to extract value, rather than duplicating familiar methods (this requires strong

leadership in line management of a business area – educate and excite them first).
- Test the requirements at every stage in the cycle. Prototype wherever possible and create model office environments for people to engage very early. Expectation management is critical to the ultimate assessment of success.
- Have a pragmatic approach to regulatory and compliance needs. Don't let the programme take all the future needs and keep them to a 'must automate' only level.
- Place all people together in one team for the period of requirements definition. One physical location is highly desirable.
- Use workshops to gain mutual understanding and co-ownership.
- Go to the workplace to understand the business processes in action. People who are making changes should watch, listen and if possible, do the work.
- Quantity is not the measure of a job well done. Concise, clear definition focusing on the business needs is preferable to a book of ideas and solutions.

"On reflection, insisting they change the systems to our old processes wasn't that clever. We ended up doing it all twice"

operations manager

Innovation or proven

This is a question that stimulates many debates and there is no straightforward answer. The right thing to do is based on the situation, the people, the risk, and the benefit.

Innovation can be valuable to gain a competitive advantage, to solve problems or for temporary solutions. But a new untried solution brings with it some risk, and the calculation and mitigation of those risks is an important companion to innovation.

The right skills and attitudes are also required to design innovative solutions. In order to innovate we often need to work in a creative, iterative environment where everything is challenged and anything is possible. There are many techniques for developing innovative solutions. The most popular in these change management experiences was to use a tailored workshop environment with professional facilitation.

Proven solutions are obviously a safer bet and should be considered when there is a need for certainty in time and cost, and ease of support and maintenance.

The story in the people chapter (8) of this book states the importance of teams but could also be used to demonstrate the pros and cons of innovation versus proven solutions in a change programme.

Simple solutions

The messages here are all about simplicity. Simple design helps delivery, understanding, implementation, training, documentation, future enhancements, support... everywhere. Complexity is often introduced for personal rather than commercial reasons. In some sectors or cultures complexity is valued, as it is deemed to reflect intelligence. I have found very few examples where this is true when delivering programmes.

"It turned out that one package release upgrade would have satisfied 80% of the function we were trying to develop"

project manager

Here are some key messages about simplifying design wherever possible:

- Choose proven solutions as a starting point – it's usually cheaper, faster, and lower risk. Innovate when you can afford to.
- Use 'out of the box' solutions where possible. Implement them to deliver 80% of scope and change them later if justifiable.
- Change the business processes to meet the systems solutions where possible. This will be cheaper and more sustainable in the long term but may be difficult to convince the business area of the value – educate and excite about the possibilities before enforcing a decision.
- Ensure future roles are understood and prepared for in any solution design. Some areas may have different responsibilities and will find it harder to accept the change if this comes as a surprise later on.
- Be rigid about standardisation and stick to agreed blueprints. Often, non-adherence is to do with preference rather than need. If ignored, the solution may not be right, particularly in terms of flexibility – don't be afraid to re-think a solution rather than blindly drive to the end with the wrong result.
- Don't allow re-invention of the wheel – some systems developers love it and will try to convince you of its worth, but from a commercial point of view won't be able to. Educate them and remind the 'prima donnas' of the business case and programme objectives (technological brilliance will not be one of them). Reward clever and simple solutions, not technically complex ones.
- Design deliverables in as small chunks as possible whilst staying efficient.
- Instigate fast decision making achieved by good governance and leadership – create a culture of accountability and trust and operate these at the right levels, not by the most senior person or through umpteen committees.
- Reward, publicise and encourage behaviours that use the *simple solutions* approach.

"The developers said they could deliver all the business needs cheaper than a package solution. If I hadn't stopped them half way, they'd still be doing it now"

project manager

Pareto's 80/20 rule

Pareto's principle is almost worth a section on it's own. A phrase I heard once is perhaps a little emotive but makes the point well: *'the pursuit of perfection is the devil's work'.* Perfection costs time and money and is unnecessary in most commercial programmes and rarely increases benefits. But let's keep this simple; applying the 80/20 principle wherever possible will ensure the maximum value from the function you design.

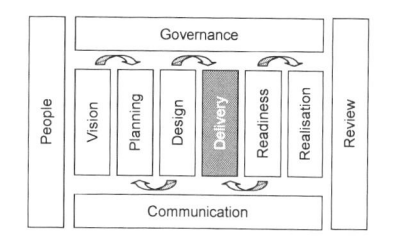

4

Delivery
Where heroes are made

Topics include:
- Building momentum
- Estimating
- Environment management
- Handover
- Cost management
- Time boxing

4: Delivery
Where heroes are made

If you get everything else right then delivery will take care of itself – but of course you don't get everything else right. So delivery has to cope with surprises and faults, making it a titanic task to achieve plans. This is where heroes are made.

The Portacabin posse – friends for life
by a programmer.

It couldn't have been a worse situation if you'd have written it for a developer's nightmare. But I look back at this experience as one of the greatest in my career.

First the background. The programme was a migration of HR and Financial systems to a vendor solution. This was as a result of a company merger and I was part of a small UK development team who was now part of a global IT function. The migration decision had been made as part of an overall standardisation to a single platform. I understood the logic but our existing systems worked, were cheap, and that's where all our skills and knowledge were. We were a young team, with minimal experience and many of us were still on our training programmes. Our task was to develop the migration programmes from our systems to the new packages. We received crash courses in the packages and were set the usual targets that were given to acquired companies. Everything was formulaic and non-negotiable. The trouble is, not one of us had been through something like this before. We didn't have the skills, the tools, the support, or the incentive. We weren't set up for success. Our motivation was the threat of failure and it's repercussions for our emerging careers.

Our manager was doing his best to support us but it was obvious he was not happy as he'd not been involved in decisions and felt exposed. Nevertheless we ploughed on and started the conversion mapping exercise. Everything was done manually and we didn't have any tools, that I now know would have been invaluable for speed and quality. We started writing the hundreds of conversion programmes that were required. The lack of systems capacity and machine priority slowed us down and we had long periods of 'downtime' waiting for results. There wasn't a test team so we tested each other's work. There wasn't any documentation or an audit team so we were the quality control and process checkers. We were doing ok but early on we were several weeks behind schedule with very few options other than to work longer hours. We worked weekends and started the days earlier and finished later. To make things worse we were isolated from the incoming new team and as space became cramped, we were moved to a Portacabin in the car park. Winter was coming and it was cold and dark. You're probably wondering why we stayed but for most of us this was our first job and we didn't have the confidence to jump ship.

Once in the Portacabin we started to create our own environment. We had the usual young lads pictures on the walls. We played music most of the time, unless someone needed a period of intense concentration. We played games during the downtime, like football with the blow-up globe or flap the fish with cut-outs from programme listings (it was a long time ago). We had accounts set up with all the local take-aways and installed a small fridge. We got very creative in ways to amuse ourselves, and the fun factor just climbed higher and higher. It was back to student digs days and our friendships were flourishing. The banter was superb. The Portacabin became our home and social centre as well as our workplace. Unknowingly, we had built an exceptionally strong team who were all pulling together for a single aim. We were self-supporting, self-coached, self-learning, and self-motivated. Our manager even moved in with us and played a valuable role of being the single conduit between the outside world and us. So we didn't need to write progress reports or escalate issues or ask difficult questions. That made us even more insular and stronger as a team.

Of course this situation had its down sides. The number of hours we were doing was phenomenal and sometimes we would work through the night, go home for a few hours sleep and back into work again. This took its toll on relationships, including mine. My girlfriend finally got fed up with only seeing me get in and out of bed and using her flat as a hotel... I got dumped. One person was absent from the final days of a relative's death through a terminal illness. One person became very ill through exhaustion and was out of action for weeks. I've heard people talk of burnout many times since but always think, "that's nothing, you should have been there in that Portacabin".

Progress was being made and there was light at the end of the tunnel. We were going to deliver late and there were going to be errors, but under the conditions this was going to be a remarkable achievement from such an inexperienced, unsupported team. We were getting very little recognition other than from messages from our manager who we all believed was inventing praise to make us feel better. It was something else that was keeping us going. The environment was addictive. The cause had been lost and no-one really remembered why we were doing it. But the loyalty to each other was incredible and no-one wanted to let the others down. As an aside, we all earned more than we did for years to come through the overtime payments and no time to spend it.

When the project came to an end we were at a loss as to what to do next. We were split up into other teams and given trainee positions. Our manager left the company and over time so did most of us, once we had completed our formal training. I've not since experienced any work as challenging as the migration project. At times we felt quite superior to others, as we knew we had been through an amazing experience together and one that they hadn't. I made some great friends who I still see today and one was best man at my wedding. This is the first time I've ever analysed the experience in terms of learning and its clear to me that we by-passed many management courses and learned more through experience than we could have done any other way.

This story is even exhausting to read. The positive experiential learning is significant. The best practices include:

- The single location helped create a close team.
- The single goal allowed total focus on delivery.
- There was great determination in adversity.
- They personalised their environment, making it more fun and more productive.
- The removal of 'noise' tasks by the manager allowed focus on their goal without distraction.

The team made heroes of themselves in their own eyes, despite not receiving the ongoing or final recognition for their efforts. But the negative experiences are also good learning:

- They were blindly running as fast as they could to the finishing post, ignorant of the personal and overall project consequences.
- There were no formal reviews.
- There was no engagement with the customer and therefore no ability to assess any changed requirements or impacts of other activities (that's good and bad!).
- There were no formal quality checks so no learning from errors.
- There wasn't any investment in tools, which in some cases can save a lot of time and money.

- There were no progress meetings to share best practice or prioritise tasks within a slipping schedule.
- There were no structured roles to utilise strengths of individuals.
- The leadership had disappeared and the manager became an administrator, which is a huge risk to morale.
- There were no experts or experienced developers to support the trainees. This would have saved a lot of time on some tasks.

I could go on... but the biggest observation for me is the extraordinary effort you can get from a team that is motivated to achieve their goal.

For the rest of this chapter we explore further some of the learning from the story and some additional areas of best practice from the experiences in the research. Systems development is still a relatively young industry and in many companies suffers from a reputation for expensive non-delivery. Every development shop has its strengths and weaknesses but there are some trends reported from developers in large and complex business programmes.

Momentum

Success breeds success and failure or delay can become a habit. It's important to get some early wins and market them hard to build momentum from the start.

> *"I looked across at the joy on their faces and how pumped up they all were through their successful delivery and thought, 'I want some of that'"*
>
> *IT developer*

Sometimes we're so busy doing the job that we forget to tell everyone about what's gone well, but as soon as something goes wrong then it spreads very quickly. Success really is contagious and it just feels so good. At one software house I visited in California they used this to good effect. They re-formed teams all the time to ensure they always had team members fresh from success, irrespective of where they were in the life cycle. Successful teams would celebrate hard, but always make it visible to others in the organisation. They would have award ceremonies, public handing out of gifts, and other methods of recognition that would make people aspire to be in a successful team. They avoided the risks of elitism and smugness by re-organising teams regularly. This gave everyone the chance to be in a successful team on a regular basis and kept the euphoria and hunger continually high. It also encouraged a competitive environment that was supportive.

Estimating

The top 3 types of development that are most under-estimated are:

1. Data migrations. They are almost always more complex than you think, always overrunning on time and cost. This should be allowed for in the estimates in plans and budgets.
2. The quality of data in legacy systems is almost certain to be poorer than anticipated. The appropriate tools and experienced resource need to be applied. Pragmatic decisions need to be made by senior business people to avoid lots of work on extreme cases with small populations e.g. pay 10 customers to transfer from an old financial product rather than build specific complex data mapping programmes.
3. Learning is usually missed from estimates and plans. In a large and complex programme there is likely to be some learning of new tools, processes, methods, or business

products and rules. If we are learning along the way then the cost and time needs to be accommodated in the plans.

In delivery you often find that many assumptions were wrong and some surprises occur. It should not be a surprise that these things usually take longer than anticipated because we have a lot of historical data to support it. Section 10 deals with the Review phase but in case you don't read it then I'll make one point again here. Spend some time at the beginning of the programme and the beginning of each stage reviewing data from previous programmes. It gives you the ammunition to make allowances in the plan that may be unpalatable but will prevent over-run. Show the programme board and other stakeholders what has happened in the past and what you are doing to mitigate the same risks, but also use the experience to revise the plan. Remember, short cuts at any stage are very likely to cost more in later stages.

Environment management

Managing all the different physical environments to support multiple versions of applications in systems development is always more complex than anticipated. Experts should be used from the start to develop a strategy with proven processes and tools and with discipline around implementation.

"How many people does it take to manage over 30 software and data environments? One... so why did it take a near mutiny to appoint him"

software delivery manager

It amazes me how many times programmes are under prepared for having the right environments, change control and data management. On one programme I was involved in it took multiple delays and an overspill of frustrated developers and testers before it was addressed. It wasn't the competence of anyone in the preparation and management of environments that was the problem; it was the lack of organisation. The management team finally agreed to hire an experienced person whose sole job was to organise the many environments required by the programme and ensue the right data and software version was on the right rig at the right time. Sounds simple, but this particular programme had over 30 rigs to manage each requiring a complete environment. The cost of the individual was low but the cost saving on productivity was massive.

Handover

This activity is often left to the end and with little planning. Delivery success will be very short lived if the support areas have insufficient material to support the change. Some of the top tips from experience of handover activity are:

- Handover plans should be written early in each project with an allowance for budget and resource.
- Capability should be developed during the programme. Coaching, mentoring, buddying, training, etc.
- Documentation is not a luxury. Keep it to essentials only and write it early and of high quality. This is often the support function's first experience of the change and will create an impression of the professionalism and quality of the programme.
- Formal 'handshakes' to all support areas must take place to ensure support functions do not feel dumped on by the programme.
- Training, education and cultural change should happen during the programme and be reviewed throughout.

In all programmes, handover is an important activity to plan for and execute well. But where external resource has been used in delivery, it is absolutely critical. I have seen many examples where costs have been tight at the end of delivery and there has been an understandable urge to remove the consultants and contractors as soon as possible. However, if their expertise and knowledge goes with them then it will be even more expensive to get them back in later to fix problems or make essential enhancements. Although not too prevalent, there are some third parties who have been known to keep back information so that they can renew their contract later in the programme or after implementation. With large organisations the handover should be part of a fixed price contract. With smaller firms or contractors there should be allowance in the length of contract, expectations made up front and then good management of knowledge throughout the contract. This is where a buddy can take responsibility and relieve the project manager of the overhead.

> *"The resource manager insisted all the contractors left as planned, but they had all the knowledge. Guess what… when they were asked back we were held to ransom"*
>
> *project manager*

In programmes where the handover issues are between organisational divides then this becomes political and there are potential walls that are built between developers, testers, support teams and users. Handover negligence is not as obviously costly with in-house teams, but imagine the impact on other programmes if their experts are brought in to help with testing, training or support calls. An effective method to ensure that handover is completed to the right quality at each stage of a programme is to use the concept of gateways. To move from one gateway to another there must be a set of criteria that is met. Knowledge transfer and documentation are two gateway criteria that, if met, will result in a positive handshake between stages and no cost, time or quality surprises further on.

Cost Management

The best delivery people are not always the best cost managers. Their single-minded approach to deliver *'at all costs'* is an admirable quality, but shouldn't be taken literally. Here are some good practices extracted from the book's research:

- Employ a project accountant and administrators with teeth, preferably in a project office.
- Track every change and hold people accountable for budgets at all levels.
- Don't let financial reporting changes interfere – if currency or rules change then keep the ability to report back to the original business case as well as adopt the changes.
- Contingency should be held mainly centrally, only allowing the projects to hold contingency in line with agreed policy e.g. for IT changes - 30% at analysis stage, 5% at coding stage.
- The amount of contingency should reflect the risk e.g. new technology, major organisational change.
- Invest in automation and new tools if they pay back within the project, or share the cost with the overall portfolio. Ensure training and familiarisation is factored into the cost.
- Post implementation support should be budgeted for within a project prior to handover to support functions. Acceptance criteria should be written early in the project and budgets agreed on both sides.

Most of the cost issues in a programme materialise within the delivery stage, but in many cases it is too late to address them fully, just minimise the impact. The planning and/or design stages are where the preventative work can be done. The bullets above describe actions that should be taken to ensure that the delivery estimates are as accurate as they can be and that the usual omissions are allowed for.

A good project accountant is worth their weight in gold. They need to be experienced in project management in order to fully understand and manage the finances of a large programme. They need to have authority and are often members of the programme board. The project managers need to see the accountant as having the voice and authority of the programme director and be managed by the accountant throughout the programme with regard to costs and benefits. The accountant needs to be at the side of the programme director and ensure they are kept honest. I remember in a programme board meeting presenting some costs when my project accountant interjected and said "I think what he meant to say was... ". Apart from being a little embarrassing, this intervention prevented me from reporting on a cost saving that wasn't there and one the board would have expected to be delivered. The accountant gave the cost and benefit reports in future board meetings.

"The project accountant was a real pain in the neck, not only for being a terrier but because it was impossible to hide anything from her. The board loved her"

project manager

The issue of contingency is always a sensitive subject. Stakeholders always try and reduce it and programme managers always try and increase it. Using historical data should help agree the right percentage. The biggest learning I had was to not give up the contingency to each project or stage - they will use it all, and possibly ask for more. Each project should be recorded exactly how it performed, whether that be over or under time or budget. As well as holding people accountable, this is the only way that future projects and programmes can learn. If contingency is always handed out then it will be difficult to track the issues and recognise the right people.

Time Boxing

Delivery to plan will be tough, even with good scope management, design, and use of the 80/20 principle. Time boxing is a good method to ensure plans are hit but with the added risk of poor quality costing dearly in testing. It's not always appropriate, but with the right team in the right circumstances, it can be beneficial. Here are some ways of reaping the benefits:

"Time boxing was unpopular at first but soon bred a culture of 'delivery at all cost' through most of the team. Some couldn't hack it and were moved"

project manager

- Create a culture of completing on time every time, even for small tasks, throughout the programme. It can become a great habit.
- Every individual must be held accountable for their own delivery and the delivery of their team.
- No-one goes home until the task is finished, tomorrow we can rest.
- Reward fairly and appropriately by making it personal and individual e.g. understand home considerations and thank partners for support with time or financial compensation.
- Keep focus on scope, simplification and the 80/20 rule. This will keep poor quality, at the expense of time and cost, to a minimum.
- Ensure there is a budget for meaningful rewards and compensation for delivering on time when unreasonable.
- Communicate this culture up front, particularly stressing that quality is not an alternative but still important. Try and only use those who 'sign up' to the agreement in advance.

I am in two minds about time boxing because it isn't right for every programme or every person. But it's in here because it can be so effective and build real momentum in the delivery stage when under pressure. If scope and quality is the most important thing in a programme, such as regulatory compliance or complex financial calculations, then it is probably not a good idea. In these circumstances, getting it just right is of paramount importance. If a product launch date is the most critical goal of the programme, having already been publicly announced, then it may be appropriate to sacrifice some scope in order to meet the date. In this case, time boxing is one good way of achieving this. So, weigh up the pros and cons first before pressing the very hot button.

Project Management

It has been said many times that everything comes down to good project management – the success or failure of the programme is totally dependent on it.

> *"I put a novice project manager on the least critical area. This is now my biggest headache and likely to be the only project that is irrecoverable"*
>
> *programme manager*

There are many ingredients to a successful programme but it is certainly true that without good project management the programme will fail. It is often a weak area if the size and complexity of programme is new territory to the organisation. There are many excellent books on project management so I'll just skim the surface here by highlighting some of the key comments made in the research:

- Recruit appropriately from specialist agencies and ensure there is flexibility in contracts (permanent or temporary) to act quickly if skills or behaviours don't fit.
- If consultants are used then introduce a buddying arrangement with internal talent and handover when skills and experience for the role are adequate. Some good consultants can do mentoring or coaching to ensure delivery and development of individuals are both achieved.
- If project managers aren't of proven calibre and experience then the programme will fail. There is no room for trying out new project managers on mission critical projects unless there is sufficient support planned in.
- Dependency management within the programme's projects and with other programmes needs constant focus.

Interestingly, these comments are saying pretty much the same thing but come from people in different types of programme roles. There was a consistent theme that the quality of project managers used on programmes was often less than what was required. Many of the delivery teams and stakeholders felt let down by this and agreed that it is the worst area to skimp on experience and skills. Some organisations insisted on professional project management qualifications before allowing sole responsibility for projects and others supplemented this with extensive behavioural analysis and psychometric testing. The role of project manager, not to be confused with project administrator (who manages Gantt charts and writes reports), is recognised as the critical element of the delivery of change.

Downsizing

The reduction in numbers of people is a common challenge that is one of the easiest changes to define on paper but often the most difficult to deliver. Section 8 discusses the issues of people in detail, but here are simple guidelines, based on experience, that will minimise the disruption and pain of delivering the less palatable type of people change:

- Implement early and quickly. Take the pain as early as possible and move into the future state as soon as you can.
- Be fair and be able to demonstrate the reasons for any decision. Be very prepared with legal and behavioural issues.
- Communicate thoughts as well as facts and be clear which is which. Most people respect the honesty and appreciate early warning or likelihood of impacts.
- Pilot in a small area first if possible and learn from the experience.
- If there are to be casualties then sometimes it is better to be apparently ruthless to be kind. Death by a thousand cuts is painful. Bring out the guillotine, use it quickly, and then burn it publicly (but don't ever use that language!).

Although speed and clarity of change are important, there are times when a more considered approach should be taken. This is when there is a deep cultural shift that is being made. Under these circumstances a quick organisation change will get immediate tangible benefits and achieve some goals but is likely to unravel as time goes on. The expression "the change journey starts in the past" is one I try and remember and is explored further in chapter 8.

5

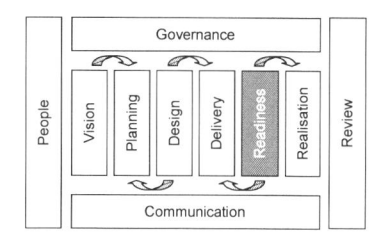

Readiness
What's the customer say?

Topics include:
- Emotional readiness
- Expectation management
- Capability
- Testing the right things
- Training and timing
- Automation tools

5: Readiness
What's the customer say?

Before we ask whether or not we are ready, I think we should address the question "who is the customer that we are preparing our readiness for?" Of course there are many customers of a change programme: sponsors, shareholders, regulators, programme people, all of who are discussed elsewhere in this book. For the purpose of this section our customer is the person who is most impacted by the change, the person whose daily life is changed through new processes, systems, and culture. This ranges from the manager who has to deliver the benefits, to the team leader who has to introduce the change, to the 'user' who actually performs the tasks.

The question "what's the customer impact?" should be used more often than any other phrase (apart from maybe "is this adding to the benefits?"). Without total engagement, support and involvement of the customer then the end result is almost certainly going to be failure. Customers need to be involved in *scope* for expectation management, *design* for usability, *delivery* for readiness, *testing* and *training* and *implementation planning* and so on… throughout the programme.

The lady who cared too much
by an operations team leader

I really didn't want to make this change. I enjoyed my job and had a real affinity with my customers. They are the elite among the group and I felt proud to provide them the best customer service in the industry. My product knowledge was strong and I had an intimate relationship with the key customers, often on first name terms.

When we were first told of the multi-brand approach, my heart sunk. In some ways I understood the logic of the efficiency gains and cost reduction but I became very protective towards my customers. I didn't want any Tom, Dick, or Harry dealing with them. I was certain that the short term cost savings would be outweighed by the loss of business through dissatisfied customers over the long term. What's more I would have to deal with the mass market. I don't want to sound snobby but it's a very different experience and it didn't appeal at all. We also had a lot of visual brand advocacy with marketing material, banners and everything in the brand colours, including the walls.

The change programme started well with focus groups that analysed the differences in the products, the service levels, the systems and processes. We all had a chance to input and were being listened to. Everything was documented and I felt we represented our customers' wishes very well. Maybe things weren't going to be so bad.

We then got involved in defining the requirements for the changes to ensure that all the multi-brand processes included the individual brands needs. In hindsight it was quite naïve to think that everything would be included, as there would be minimal efficiency gains if we replicate everything. Unfortunately we didn't get involved in the prioritisation session that slashed half of what we needed. As feared, the focus was on minimum service levels and numbers, and not on genuine customer care. When it came to signing off the final version of the requirements I stated my concerns for our customers but felt under huge pressure to sign the document. I'm sure they left me until last for that very reason. The 'lesser' brands would get some extra features and we would lose some of ours. I reluctantly signed.

Everything went quiet for a few months and many of us pretended it had gone away. Maybe they came to their senses and maybe some new management had reversed the decision? Then I was asked to free up some of my team for testing. The feedback was horrific. Even more of our requirements had been removed. The systems and processes looked completely different and half of what we asked for wasn't there. The focus of the testing was on what worked and not what was needed to service the customer. On this basis, again, we reluctantly signed off the testing. The training went the same way, as did the documentation. Technically, the programme was going really well. Everything worked, we were all trained on how to use the new systems and processes, and we had comprehensive documentation and on-line support. The other brands thought it was the best thing they ever had.

I was asked to sign off the readiness document. This was the final stage before putting the changes into our daily lives – the nail in the coffin. It was presented as a done deal because it was impossible not to tick all the boxes. There was no question about end customer readiness or colleague advocacy. Physically, things looked similar on the outside and technically everything worked. Organisationally, there were minimal changes with the threat of more to come in the future once the new systems and processes had bedded in. So was I ready? Technically yes, emotionally no.

The programme was deemed a great success as it achieved its cost benefits and was a reasonably smooth implementation. The preparation was as good as it had ever been in terms of systems and process change. The impact of not being emotionally bought in to the changes was not apparent at first but after a while a few things started to bite. The team weren't volunteering for the over time that was required to do the manual workarounds needed because of systems errors. 'Day 2' promised to fix some customer experience issues but no sign of when. Service levels were degraded for my brand, as the new people didn't know how to talk to the customers, what language to use and when to go off script. Their knowledge of the products was worse than the customer and we started to get complaints. Sales for the brand dipped.

We're now undertaking a brand recovery project and have temporarily moved all the experienced people back together, albeit with less tools. All the right noises are being made over cultural change and customer care, but I'm not sure if it's too late.

I find this story a little sad. The programme was very well executed for everything it intended to do but it missed out a major part of readiness. The emotional readiness is critical to getting the hearts and minds of colleagues aligned with the changes and prepared to accept imperfections. The key learning from this story can be split into good and bad practice. The programme was a success in the following respects:

- A strong vision based on the need for efficiency gains.
- Good planning and execution of all systems and process change.
- Initial programme launch workshops involving all areas affected.
- Requirements workshops involving all brands.
- Comprehensive testing, training and documentation (although they only testing that it worked, not what was promised)
- Communication of benefits realised.

The programme felt like a failure to those who weren't ready for the change because of a few critical points:

- Scope management communication was poor when prioritisation occurred and function dropped out.

- Expectation management was poor and there were surprises during a vacuum of user involvement during the build stage.
- Failure to identify and address elitism and the impact of cultural change to one brand.
- Failure to recognise the lack of emotional buy-in from one brand's colleagues.

The remainder of this chapter describes further learning from experiences related to readiness.

Expectation management

The business areas receiving the change must be fully prepared and be enthused about it. These are two different things. The story told earlier in this section shows how critical emotional readiness is, even if all the practical elements are delivered. Expectation management is a key element to achieving emotional buy-in.

It's a lot easier to over promise in order to get through difficult discussions over programme issues, such as scope management or schedules. But this is where many of the customers' programme advocacy issues start.

Even with involvement there is likely to be a difference of opinion of the final outcome, of how the change will look and feel and what impact it will have. It will also change throughout the programme so a true understanding of each others position needs to be kept current. Typically there will be compromise and risks that need to be bought into and owned by the customer so that there is not a feeling of 'being done to'.

Not all change will be good to all people. This is where being honest with some difficult messages early on is critical to the readiness process. Not everyone will be an advocate of the changes but realism is important to prevent them becoming saboteurs. The vision needs to be clear, not only from a group perspective, but right down to an individual. Being ready for a change starts with knowing exactly what is expected.

Capability

Once there is a good understanding of how everyone will be impacted by the change the next question is "do we have the capability to manage the change?" Capability is partly the skills and knowledge required to adapt to the processes, roles and tools, to prepare for what is being delivered by the programme.

> *"We had a re-organisation, a systems upgrade, some new documentation and now a revamp of the products. They'll need to change my brain next"*
>
> *operations team leader*

Capability is also pertinent to the current state of the business area. For example, the business area may have the technical skills and knowledge to do the preparatory work but may not have the resource availability during a peak period of activity. There may also be some other changes in the area that require similar preparation. Here's some of the key learning from other programmes:

- Ensure there is a change portfolio approach to each business area. For example, keep a change calendar and resource plan, which will quickly highlight capability risks.
- Involve business areas impacted early and fully in every stage. Plan for the change preparation in their budgets and resource plans.
- Educate, educate, educate. Things will be very different during and after the programme. Life will be different, so the people need to get used to it before it happens to them.

- Use a model office where possible and use good communication techniques that bring the change to life before it happens (see chapter 9).
- Re-engineer processes where needed for the programme, but don't use this change as an opportunity to change everything. Scope management in business areas is as important as in the programme delivery.
- Develop change capability expertise in each department, often the system and process specialist. Part of their time needs to be allocated to the programme but should not attempt to replace a project manager role.
- Employ a business change expert if required, but not one who turns up with new models and theory. Practical change implementation experience is required to prepare for large programme change. The expert needs to drive the change through the managers and not be the demon of change that has only a short-term impact.

Testing

After managing expectations and establishing capability we now move onto checking whether the change actually works and whether it meets the expectations set during the vision and design stages. This is not the right publication to discuss the intricacies of systems and user acceptance testing strategies. However, it's worth noting that there are some consistent themes from this stage of a programme that need highlighting.

"Test environments are never there when we need them. It's soul destroying for all the testers and users"

testing manager

The most common experiences are:

- Test environments are rarely available to users when they should be.
- User testing often gets squeezed due to the unavailability of test environments or the quality of data in them.
- Test environments' data doesn't reflect the live production environment, so anomalies are often missed.
- There are often configuration issues between different environments that can cause an abnormally high level of performance issues either during testing or after implementation.
- Error management is done well, with good categorisation and reporting of defects.
- There is little ownership of issues arising from testing and time is wasted debating where the fault lies rather than fixing it.
- Business areas are pressured into accepting errors and categorising them as low impact.

Many of the issues described above are due to the often-neglected challenge of test environment management. Where there are a large number of environments required, a test environment planning role needs to be created and filled with a strong manager. Testing is being considered more of a profession these days so ensure your team members are qualified, experienced, and have the right tools and methods.

Quality Management

It's obviously important that the quality of the programme's output is tested and meets expectations. It's also pretty obvious that the quality of the changes made in the business areas affected need equal focus. But one thing that is often over looked is the regression testing against any quality management system that exists, either in a total business or in one or more business areas. I remember one company who invested heavily in total quality management (TQM), covering organisation, operating processes, products, and services. They blamed a major programme, which was in itself highly successful, for not being able to meet the requirements of their TQM.

Most organisations are going to have one form of quality measure whether it be TQM, or a recognised standard that begins with BS or ISO, or simply a set of service levels (with external and internal customers). The testing against these measures needs to be a part of the programme readiness stage. It needs to be planned and budgeted for and resources allocated.

"I happily banked the programme delivery bonus like everyone else, but I'd give that up for the money I'll lose through missing service levels"

operations administrator

Training

The most consistent theme from the experiences people have with training for change is not the quality but the timing. In many instances the training is scheduled and delivered irrespective of the ever-changing demands on the people and the moving dates of the programme. Even an excellent training course will be mostly forgotten if it is attended way in advance of the skills being used. It is also frustrating for people if the content of the training doesn't match what is being delivered to them in reality. Training environments need to reflect the production environment or there will be productivity loss through queries and lack of confidence.

This is a particularly difficult issue in business areas where people's time is measured to the minute because they are a part of a big department striving to meet productivity targets and service levels. A call centre is the classic environment where scheduling for training is a massive overhead and, when dates move, can be a logistical nightmare. They cannot afford to do the training twice, they cannot afford to lose productivity through under-skilled people and they cannot afford the overtime when it goes wrong. Training plans need to be integrated with resource plans and kept current all the time. When a programme is planned, the business areas should consider the additional capacity required and the flexibility required to avoid disruption to their business.

> *"The training was excellent. I was ready to use my new skills and knowledge. Sadly, it was several weeks before the changes came and I'd forgotten most of it"*
>
> operations administrator

The need for different training styles is also spoken about as an issue in the readiness stage. A different style is required for different types of change. For example, one company used workshop training for all their programmes, which usually worked well. People liked the interactive nature and the classroom approach where they could work in teams, ask questions and most important of all, try things out. But there were two issues.

Firstly, they forgot a lot of what they learned and needed somewhere to try it out. A model office was considered too expensive and the business managers didn't want to release the teams for any additional training. Secondly, there were product changes that needed to be learned. Introducing them in the classroom was useful but because everyone learns at a different pace, some people wanted to do some homework or be given more time to remember the detail. The documentation was good as a reminder but not as learning material. Again, this was considered an unnecessary overhead.

Most people dealt with the changes well and after an initial dip in productivity got back up to speed and in fact met the increase in targets that were part of the benefit realisation. But for some, they struggled to meet targets and were downgraded in their performance. They were previously solid performers and this impacted theirs and others morale, ultimately causing the cost of replacing some of them. With more time and the facility to go back and re-learn some of the details, perhaps also with time allocated to buddying, the overall change would have been received smoother.

Personal Development Plans

A big assumption here is that everyone impacted by the change programme will have a personal development plan (PDP). It is likely to be called a number of different things but is simply an agreement between a colleague and their manager as to what development they will be undertaking in a given period. The development will be linked to the team, department and organisation goals so they can see how they contribute to the wider picture. The development will also be linked to their own personal aspirations whether that is for technical excellence or career advancement. In addition to all this, the PDP must have reference to the training required to be ready for the changes from the programme. If not, it will appear to be less important and of less value to their development. Making the links between the programme training and the PDP will result in a more enthusiastic recipient of the training and one who understands how it will benefit themselves and the company.

Tools

The use of tools could really be included in every section of this guide. But there was a surprisingly little amount of comment from surveys and interviews regarding the significance of tools in change programmes. There are many tools available for almost every aspect of a programme, from vision through to realisation.

The general consensus is that tools can make things quicker and easier and is some cases improve quality. For example, data mapping software for system conversion programmes can take a lot of grunt work away and improve speed and quality as well as reduce cost. However, they also require a great deal of investment. The tools with the biggest gain are usually the ones that have the biggest capital outlay and largest training time and cost. This leads us to the clearest message coming from the research regarding tools. If possible, do not use mission critical programmes to try out new tools. If you can see a genuine significant net benefit in using a new tool then allow for the cost and time in the planning stage. Even then, it will inevitably cost you more than you save for the current programme.

I remember working on a long and complex systems infrastructure replacement programme. There was a huge amount of regression testing to be done and we hired some new expertise to manage the different phases of testing required. The new manager recommended some market leading tools. The business case was excellent, with immediate pay back in the programme and ongoing benefits for future programmes. The testing teams were highly motivated to learn the new tools, get a certification, and make their lives easier and their work more interesting. The investment didn't even need departmental authorisation as the programme could justify the expense because of the net benefit.

"We invested in people and tools and probably had as good a testing capability as anyone in our industry. Trouble is, we neglected delivering for the programme"

project manager

The testing phase took an immediate hit on the timeline because of the resource required to do the training. Then the productivity was very low, as the familiarisation period was needed. Then there were the errors caused by inexperience with the tool. Then there was the utilisation reduction caused by the one or two experienced people being used for assisting the novices. At the end of the testing phase we had a team of testers who had been through the mill and come out with some great experience of new tools and earned some qualifications. The quality of testing ended up very high for what was a complex set of scenarios. But... we over ran on time and budget which could not be recovered at such a late a stage in the programme. The tools were an excellent investment for future programmes but were a big mistake for this one. Picking the right programme and the right time to introduce new tools is critical.

Lonely Project

6

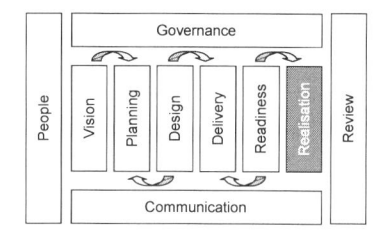

Realisation
Will they pay the bill?

Topics include:
- Benefit ownership
- Benefit management
- Negative benefits
- Benefit tracking
- Benefit realisation planning
- Post programme blues

6: Realisation
Will they pay the bill?

They think it's all over... it isn't. The party has been planned and delivered to perfection, the stories have started and the heroes are basking in the glory of their achievements. Many awards have been given and people can finally take their postponed holiday. But there is still one critical question needing an answer to demonstrate how successful the programme has been – "did we achieve the benefits?"

The ultimate test is whether or not the sponsor would pay the bill – did he get value for money and were all the benefits delivered? Ongoing management of the business case should make this a formality, but there is often a lot of unnecessary debate at this stage.

The battle of the benefits
by a sales director (SD) and a customer services director (CSD).

CSD – You signed up to massive income growth from the programme deliverables so that you could get new products through a new e-channel. But you knew it would be impossible to make a direct link between the programme deliverables and the benefits as there were so many other factors affecting sales.

SD – admittedly it's not easy to make a direct link but it was pretty obvious that new products would mean more sales, so it was the right thing to do. You can't get too hung up on precise measurement providing we all deliver our targets. The trouble is, you didn't deliver, and that's why we suffered in future new business.

CSD – The reason I didn't deliver service improvements was because all of my functionality got dropped in favour of your fictitious income figures. My efficiency targets may not have been as bigger numbers but at least they were real and were easy to demonstrate realisation.

SD – Look, if a systems change can generate major growth then it will always be prioritised over service. Your team can just throw more bodies at it and we'll still be more efficient through better cost/income ratios, which result in higher profits. You should try and see the bigger picture and not just the back office.

CSD – The bigger picture is about having an end-to-end service that supports the marketing and distribution. You can't just have half the solution or you get service issues that cause reputation damage and less business in the long term. The programme board didn't believe me when I said this would happen and you didn't support me.

SD – The way I'm supporting you is to ensure you get a bonus this year through achieving our growth and profit targets. Don't worry about next year, I've got some more new initiatives that will wow the market and they'll be biting our hands off for what we'll have on offer.

CSD – My god, you just don't get it do you. More new products, no more service automation, more errors, higher costs, and more complaints… you can't keep thinking about the short term or there won't be a long term. And in any case, my bonus is also based on cost and service so you are damaging any chance of me achieving an on target bonus. And, how an earth can you keep getting away with a benefit in a business case that is impossible to measure.

SD – It's because of my sales record that I am trusted to deliver in whatever way I like. I have the products and marketing boys supporting me and so should you. My targets are very measurable, every week! You see my reports and the traffic lights are always green. If you look at it holistically over a years change portfolio then I will achieve the accumulative growth of all the benefits I've signed up to. Surely, if I do that year after year then I deserve to get the investment I need. Maybe you should make a similar case and ask for more investment with a delivery promise for the year instead of the minute process management detail that you quote. No-one gets excited by the number of seconds it takes to process new business. We care about delivering the service level to our customer and that's what your business case should say.

CSD – actually it does, you just don't read it. The detail is there to support the claim of the benefit. Without that then I would have no confidence it could be achieved. I run a production environment where these measures are critical to supporting the service you are selling. My issue about your benefits are that there's no evidence to say that you wouldn't achieve your targets without all the bells and whistles. We see so many product failures and MI that's never used. I don't doubt your team's selling credentials but maybe they can do it without investment in so many new initiatives and we can get a larger slice of the pie to support our customers post sale.

SD – haven't you heard of the phrase 'speculate to accumulate'? We have to try things out and not everything will work. As I said earlier, you have to look at the bigger picture over the year. Look, I'll support you in the next prioritisation meeting and we'll make a good case for more investment in service, particularly because of the hole we're in at the moment. But I'm not going to suggest it's at the expense of my sales projects. What about all those finance projects?

CSD – Thanks, and don't start me on finance!

This conversation is quite typical and I can certainly see both sides of the argument. You have to take risks and not every idea will work, so it makes sense to see all the sales initiatives as one programme. It doesn't make sense to ignore the back office requirements to maintain customer service and these could be included in each project or as a separate programme. It demonstrates that realisation of benefits starts right at the start of structuring the programme portfolio. Personally, I've seen better benefit management and more consistent realisation when the portfolio is structured by function and therefore there is a single owner of the realisation. There is less matrix management of changes to the way benefits will be delivered but it is essential that there is interlock between the dependant parties. If the inter-relationships between programme benefits are not maintained then it is possible that no programme achieves its targets.

Some other observations, that would ease the relationship from the story and get the accountabilities clear, are:

- Understand the benefit measurement viability and be honest about it. If it's not possible to measure in isolation (such as sales) then ensure there is portfolio accountability in place i.e. across all change initiatives.
- If the benefits are subjective then, again, be open about it to avoid wasted effort trying to justify them later. Many complex pieces of MI are produced to do this and are rightly always challenged. Subjective benefits also need to be apparent in the prioritisation process.
- There is often a time-based prioritisation of scope during a programme cycle. A well-used phrase is that we tend to work on what is urgent rather than what is important. For example, service enhancements often get dropped because they can theoretically wait, but a product is essential for launch. It is

important to ensure that all the programme board members and stakeholders agree this approach at the outset of the programme. They also need to note and accept the consequences. For example, a period of non-delivery of service levels may be the consequence of de-scoping of function and the implications could also be a temporary cost overrun.
- In order to understand the different measures within an organisation, the programme stakeholders need to be educated on the business operating model. A step further would be to share the total goals of the programme, not just their area of accountability. This starts to stray into the culture of organisations and how they are rewarded, so won't be explored further here.
- Finally, never trust a salesman (joke).

"He got away with it. All his benefits were long term and then he changed job before they were realised"

benefit owner

The remainder of this chapter covers some other learning from the experiences of the realisation stage from the research.

Benefit Management

It's easy to determine the success of the delivery phases with regard to scope, cost and time. Towards the end of a programme, quality is just starting to be measurable as errors arise during the warranty period. The exit criteria are being dusted off and people are being moved onto new challenges. There will also inevitably be the initiation of smaller projects to add more function, deliver requirements that were delayed, or enhance the processes and systems in line with changing markets and strategies. The post implementation review is planned and the governance is being wound down. The one thing that needs to continue beyond the programme is benefit management.

The single most important thing to deliver is the benefits, the focus on which is often left to the end. It should be remembered that the systems, processes, architecture and organisational changes are all enablers of delivering the benefits in the business case; the reason that the programme started.

> *"We spent 6 months writing a benefit management manual only to find there was an almost identical one available in the market – what a waste of time"*

A good benefit management process needs to be adopted from beginning to end... and beyond. There are a growing number of tools and processes available now from suppliers and consultants. When selecting or developing your own benefit management system, there are some minimum requirements and outputs:

- Measurable benefits linked to strategic objectives and the programme vision.
- Commitment by benefit owners (senior stakeholders) who each have their own benefit realisation plan.
- An easy to follow benefit reporting tool that monitors by exception.
- Fluidity to allow for new or different benefits, but with a rigid change management system.
- Ability to define and measure soft and long term benefits as well as financial ones e.g. capability.

I've avoided referring to products or suppliers in this book, for two reasons. Firstly, I want to stay objective and not imply any bias that could benefit me in some way. Secondly, things change so fast in this business that today's experts could be tomorrow's has-beens. Having said that, I'm going to break the rule now because, at the time of writing, there is one organisation that I think really understands benefit management, particularly from programmes with heavy systems changes. They are Cranfield School of Management. Having given them a plug, I'll use a simple diagram of theirs to demonstrate the additional value of using benefit management. They tested 20 programmes in blue chip companies and found that for a little extra cost in using a structured benefit management process you can gain considerable additional benefits. In many cases I would suggest these are the benefits that were planned to achieve and without benefit management there would have been a significant deficit.

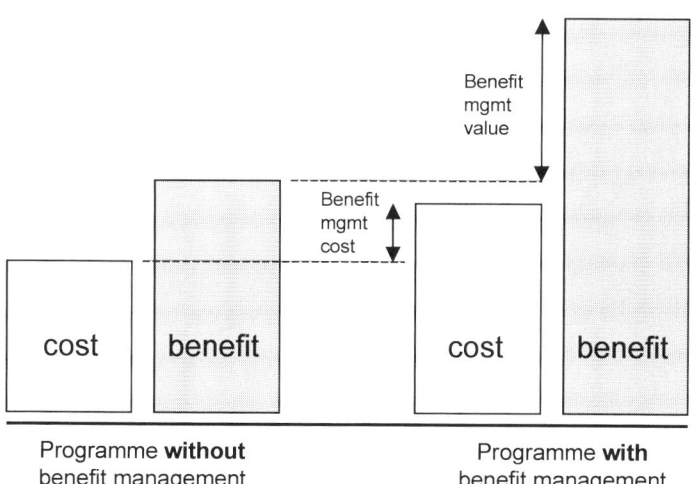

[Chart showing two bar groups: "Programme **without** benefit management" with cost and benefit bars, and "Programme **with** benefit management" with cost and benefit bars. Labels indicate "Benefit mgmt cost" and "Benefit mgmt value".]

One of the obvious benefits highlighted in the chart is the additional benefit through focus and management process. It is similar to the common expression used that you only achieve what you measure. There is evidence to show that the more focus on benefits that a stakeholder has and the more accountability they have for delivering them, then the more likely the programme will deliver the benefits, and more. The process of managing the benefits adds value in a number of ways:

- The focus on delivery becomes a focus on benefit.
- The programme outputs are linked with the business strategy and goals.
- Implementation plans become change management plans
- Business managers are engaged and active in the programme.
- Scope is rationalised to be directly contributing to benefits, potentially reducing programme costs.
- There is a clear definition of success that everyone can relate to.
- The criteria for continuing or stopping a programme is identified early and managed at every stage review.
- Portfolio management can occur with a set of common measures.
- There is a common language for risk management.

The list could go on. As I think I've pointed out more than once in this book, the benefits should be central to every decision and investment made, with a continuous review throughout the programme. You get the message now, so I'll move on.

Net benefits

In defining benefits for a programme many organisations only focus on the positive benefits.

"Most gamblers only ever tell you of their winnings and not their losses. It's like that here with stakeholder benefits... what about all the additional operating costs?"

project accountant

In most large programmes, particularly when transformational, there are also things that have to be given up, or negative benefits. Some of the more obvious ones are people costs such as redundancy or recruitment. A more subtle one may be some additional expenses associated with a change in travel behaviour following a location move e.g. hotels, video-conference facilities. It is useful to look at the cause and effect of change to understand the net benefit picture. The matrix below is an example of how to consider hard and soft benefits prior to putting them in a business case. It could avoid the embarrassment of stakeholder challenge on negative benefits that haven't previously been considered.

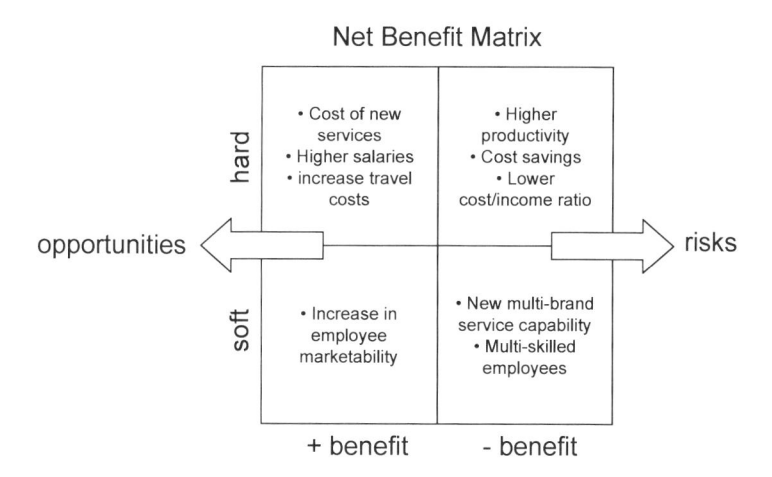

Net Benefit Matrix

	+ benefit	- benefit
hard	• Cost of new services • Higher salaries • increase travel costs	• Higher productivity • Cost savings • Lower cost/income ratio
soft	• Increase in employee marketability	• New multi-brand service capability • Multi-skilled employees

opportunities ⇐   ⇒ risks

The example shown is for a change that centralises the operational service into a single multi-brand organisation. For each change in the programme there is an outcome and an associated list of benefits. For a brainstorming session, the left hand column of positive benefits can be considered 'the cause' and the right hand column (which is often blank when transferred from a business case) is 'the effect'. As many people find negative brainstorming easier than positive, it shouldn't be too difficult to start filling out the right hand column for each programme outcome. However, a strong warning is that this could adversely impact programme advocacy. Some of the negative benefits will be risks and never materialise just as some of the positive benefits are opportunities to be stored in the back pocket for over delivery. Some of them may be unduly exaggerated and not as material as first thought. It is critical to distinguish between real benefits for the business case and risks/opportunities for the best/worse case scenarios (sensitivity analysis). Ultimately it is this analysis that may get the programme accepted or rejected by the board.

As well as helping define the net benefit picture, this exercise is a great start to the risk management process. Managing the benefit risk is the most important risk to manage and should have the full support of the programme office and programme management.

Benefit tracking

The timing of the benefit is another important aspect to get right at the outset. The end of the delivery stage is not the right place for a benefit owner to let you know that it will be two years before the benefits will be realised. This would have had a serious impact on the priority of the programme at the outset and would certainly lose much of the programme's credibility. To evidence long-term benefit realisation is a very difficult challenge in most cases, as the measures are usually impacted by more and more things over time. Also, accountability becomes more difficult when personnel or organisational changes take place mid term. A good way of avoiding the long term tracking of benefits is to ensure that benefits get added to performance measures. A benefit can be legitimately signed off as realised when there is a corresponding increment to someone's performance measures. Of course in many cases they can achieve the benefit a different way, but this is better than losing the accountability or traceability over time. Programme's can then be assessed immediately and closed (after the learning review).

The management of benefits starts right at the beginning of the programme and not at the end. The graph below demonstrates that your ability to influence the benefits reduces over time.

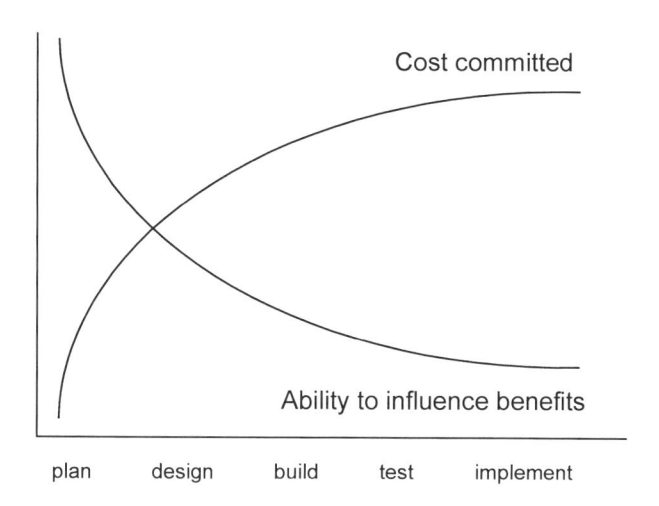

Graph showing two curves across stages plan, design, build, test, implement: "Cost committed" rising and "Ability to influence benefits" falling.

For example, if a benefit gap is identified in the testing stage then the ability to add scope to the programme to fill the gap is limited without extending the time of the programme. Any changes are also likely to cost more as a certain amount of sunk cost has been incurred and there would be a need to revisit the design as well as the delivery. This may seem an obvious statement but many people only monitor benefits towards the end of the programme when it is often too late to make changes necessary to fill benefit gaps.

A few comments on soft, or intangible benefits. Some people have the view that there should never be a stated benefit in the business case that cannot be measured. I don't fully subscribe to this but agree that the fewer of these the better. Using another cause and effect process, many soft benefits can eventually be associated with a tangible measure. For instance, customer service improvements should result in higher customer retention, which based on customer profitability models has a value. Where I don't subscribe to these chains of cause and effect is where the link has lost any traceability and is so tenuous that it can never be proved. Many people would support the view that happy people are more productive than unhappy ones. But not many would be willing to put a value on a productivity increase through a morale improvement change programme and commit to evidencing it. In organisations where their primary objectives are profit and shareholder value, most business cases are approved and prioritised on the hard benefits. The soft ones are often used as 'the joker' when deciding on priorities of programmes with equivalent financial value or ROI.

The tracking of multiple programmes' benefits into one functional set of performance measures is a critical role. This often takes place in a strategy function, a Finance function or a business change function. Irrespective of where this happens it is an important step to managing the benefit realisation of the portfolio and the alignment to the strategic objectives and business plan.

Benefit realisation planning

Without detailed planning of the benefits value and timing, it is difficult to have a credible business case and one that doesn't have a high risk of error. Every stakeholder should have a benefit realisation plan that is monitored by the project office and visible to everyone.

Here are some key points on benefit realisation planning from the experience in the research:

- It is critical to define, review, monitor and change benefit plans. A detailed benefit realisation plan is required for every business area and for every major cost.
- Use tools but don't re-invent them, they won't make you deliver the benefits. 'Off the shelf' methods and tools are widely available from external suppliers.
- Often a big culture change is required to drive out the benefits. Manage expectations up front and stick to the plans,

documenting every change and impact on the way, with programme board sign off. Try and encourage a 'benefit out – benefit in' policy which will provide flexibility on *how* benefits will be delivered and retain the ultimate value.
- There is potential to duplicate benefits across programmes or 'business as usual' activity. Ensure that cross programme benefit management is happening and that shared benefits are avoided. The argument over which programme delivered what share of benefits is rarely won.

> *"There was double counting of benefits in the portfolio and we were publicly exposed by the finance team... and ultimately absorbed by them"*
>
> *project office*

Post programme blues

There is one more task to do after the programme has completed, other than realise the benefits. The programme needs to be officially closed and that involves some people issues. One of the biggest oversights is often what to do with the programme team.

Towards the end of large, long, complex programmes, people are often functioning largely on adrenalin alone and they almost become dependent on it. So how do we feed the demand of these junkies? The period of rest is essential for their health, but soon afterwards the addicts are no longer happy with documentation and post implementation reviews. They need to be given mission critical challenging tasks to achieve. They miss the passion, emotion, team spirit and the pizza. They need to get off the habit carefully and slowly.

Some people leave an organisation after big transformation programmes if they aren't offered an opportunity to utilise their new skills and experience. As they seek to better themselves and re-create those fading memories, consultancies often benefit from the experience of the ambitious ones. This is inevitable and should be accepted as part of the cost of the programme… unless of course there is another large, complex programme around the corner.

The ability of an organisation to change is fast becoming a key competitive advantage. So we have to keep the momentum going and re-use the experience of that expanding A-team to undertake the next impossible mission.

7

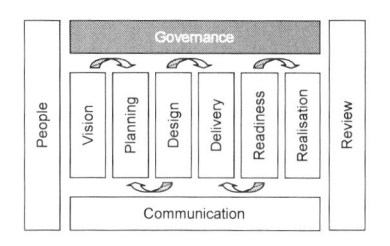

Governance
Monitoring with teeth

Topics include:
- Programme structure
- Governance roles
- Reporting
- The steering group
- The programme board
- Risk management

7: Governance
Monitoring with teeth

Governance is an unnecessary bureaucratic overhead... or at least it can be. If the people and forums are not going to be given the authority to do their jobs then don't bother with them. But without governance the programme will rely solely on individual talent, experience and a whole bunch of heroes. Then at the end, they won't know how and why they've failed. Governance with teeth is essential to delivering the business case.

The one about the polar bear
by a programme manager.

I was sitting in a lovely restaurant overlooking Edinburgh castle with the programme director. We were planning our next programme board meeting in London over a shellfish platter and a glass or two of Sancerre. All my best thinking happens in this environment! The board meeting was going to be very challenging. We had some difficult messages to give about slippage on delivery and we had some difficult decisions to make on scope and benefits. Previous programme board meetings had been fairly routine; reporting everything on track with a few risks and issues to manage. Attendance had dropped and deputies were regularly sent. The style of the meeting was getting stale and it often appeared as though we were just going through the motions. In some respects this was ok because of the good progress of the programme, but now we required senior management focus and decisions to be made with full support. We needed energetic and lively debate from all parties because some of the decisions did not have clear recommendations. Stakeholder management had been challenging because of the increasing apathy towards the programme. So we had to do something different.

As the wine flowed, we started our usual idea generation, which deteriorated into fantasy. The relationship was good and we quite often gave each other personal challenges or made bets on outcomes to spice up our days on the programme. We were a year into the programme and the initial excitement was waning and so these were great ways to relieve stress and inject energy. I don't remember who had the idea first as it was one of a string of increasingly outrageous challenges. Having failed to buy the huge painting on the restaurant wall from the owner I was not ready to be defeated on the next challenge. But before I knew it I had committed to bringing a stuffed polar bear to the next board meeting.

I woke up a little 'heady' and strolled down to breakfast and with my first sip of black coffee I remembered my challenge. My immediate thoughts were "impossible" and "I'd be fired", but my inherent competitiveness wasn't going to allow me to dismiss it so early. I started to mull over my options and amazingly there was an outside possibility of borrowing a stuffed polar bear through a contact I had. Even if I could get one, how could I justify its presence at the boardroom table? I thought about all the potential play on words, the analogies, the big punch line at the end of the meeting, and started to amuse myself all over again. It definitely had potential, so my efforts turned to the challenge of finding one.

I can't really tell you how it happened but I drove down the motorway one morning with a new passenger. I was a day early for the board meeting so needed somewhere to store it. Trouble was it was 8 foot tall and wasn't easy to hide. I looked at the boardroom schedule and luckily there were no meetings before the programme board meeting and so in he went. I stood him behind the door and hoped no-one would see him. Of course that was not going to happen.

I decided to use the polar bear to get the right attendance and focus for the meeting so I sent out a meeting invitation update. We were to have a special guest at the meeting who had enormous stature and presence. He would be impossible to ignore and would provide the additional focus we needed for a challenging meeting. All board members must attend in person and be prepared to make some tough decisions. The preparation was exemplary and all the issues, risks, and debates were well documented. But they were a secondary focus on the invitation. The attention was all on the new board member.

Now, I wasn't going to totally risk my career so involved the CEO in the stunt. I explained that we needed to attract the attention of key people and re-energise the programme board. He came into the boardroom, peered round the door, looked up (and he was 6'4") and just shook his head, leaving the room without comment – I knew that was approval!

Word got out that there was something amazing in the boardroom and people were flocking to see it. I got the room locked so the teaser campaign was well underway and the secret was kept. This was only to be revealed at the programme board meeting. The anticipation was building and I got full attendance from everyone I needed at the meeting. The programme director, who started to distance himself from the challenge, was now beginning to make noises about it being his idea and a stroke of genius.

On the day, we put the polar bear at the end of the long oak table. He was not only an intimidating figure by size but had a scary posture. His arms were raised high above his head in the attack position, making him even taller. His jaws were wide open revealing his blood stained teeth and tongue. His claws were *longer than my hands and his eyes (false, because that's the only bit that can't be preserved) were glassy and staring. I got cold feet again. How could I expect intense debate and hard decision making to go on when it could appear I was making a joke of it all? The reaction was stunning and totally unpredictable.*

As each board member came in the room, they took a glance at our new board member but didn't say a thing. They had read the meeting documentation and one or two were ready for a fight. The only verbal comment made was from someone who was late who, slightly flustered, apologised to the bear and sat down… very cool. The first thing that was different was that everyone sat in a different seat to their usual position… away from the bear. So far so good. We had full attendance, attention, and focus. We followed a more exception-based approach to the reporting such that we got to the issues very quickly. We had a robust challenge to slippage, with reluctant acceptance. We had a very lively, sometimes fiery debate on scope and priorities and benefit challenge. The CEO performed brilliantly by putting all sponsors on the spike for new benefits and a clear expectation that this is the only re-plan we were going to do and the programme team had to deliver. A great result, we even finished earlier than usual.

On the way out, everyone smiled about the polar bear and through no prior explanation or comment from the CEO, had made up their own reason for why it was there. The programme director got some credit for innovation and one simply said, "the bear was genius". Attendance at future meetings was good and we learned a lot about focusing on exceptions and decisions, about stakeholder management, about keeping it fresh. Above all, when the going gets tough, you can still have a bit of fun.

On my way home, I felt very happy with the outcome and smug about winning the bet and not having to pay for the next meal with the programme director. The story ends with me being pulled over by the police, having to explain why I had an 8 foot polar bear sticking out the roof of my car!

I love that story, and who'd have thought it would be in the boring governance section of the book. The programme manager is clear about the problem he had to solve and the learning points. The key point for me is that governance is pointless without teeth (pardon the pun). If it is a bureaucratic routine exercise then it is just an unnecessary overhead. But used as a way of managing risks and issues at the highest level, it is an essential element to delivering successful programmes. Here's a recap of other learning points from the story:

- Attendance must be from the most senior stakeholders. Empowered deputies are an allowable second best, but test how empowered they really are. My experience is that when it comes to the big decisions, the senior stakeholder wants to input or even change decisions after the meeting. This is totally unacceptable as it undermines the authority of the programme board and wastes a lot of people's time having to reconvene with the right decision makers.
- The programme board is not like some other boards where they only focus on issue management. Challenge and debate is important to determine the risks and issues that aren't yet understood. For example, external factors or changes to business plans may not be information that is available to programme teams and this is the time to ensure everything is discussed. Also, programme board members need to have a full understanding of progress and issues so that they can represent the programme outside of the meeting.
- Stakeholders and board members must make themselves available for pre-meeting debriefs. They need to be informed so that they armed with information and have had the opportunity to do their thinking. This will make for a higher quality debate and a more efficient meeting. Not many

people are comfortable with surprises and will often sabotage a debate or meeting if they feel uncomfortable or disadvantaged.
- Give people a reason to attend the meeting. This maybe being prepared for a serious debate or an opportunity to show off their performance. Whatever it is, they must come with a positive attitude, ready to be active and engage
- Report by exception. People get bored very quickly if there is nothing to do or say. Highlight achievements enthusiastically but don't dwell on the detail.

The remainder of this chapter focuses on the structure and process used in the most successful programmes from the research. There are many alternatives available and no right answers, it's more a point of knowing how and when to use them. The programme organisation discussed below was emerging as the most popular, recognising that different programmes require different focus.

Programme Structure

The diagram below is one of many varied structures that can be adopted. Indeed, programme structures can change throughout the life of a long programme as it becomes more/less complex. The important thing is that all the components exist within the structure, not who reports to who. The structure may also depend on the nature of the programme and the importance of any one area. For example, a large culture change programme may require a separate organisation development work stream, or a primarily regulatory change programme may require a legal and compliance work stream.

Although roles can mix and match it is recommended that certain skills and functions are kept separate. The delivery people should focus on just that and not be distracted by other activities. If they need resources then they go to resource management, they should not be bogged down with administrative overhead or discussions about careers – they must focus 100% on delivery. If they are given additional responsibilities, then delivery people will put them, rightly, to a lower priority and that's when things such as communication, recognition, and reporting, all fall away. Financial management may be brought out of the project office depending on skill set.

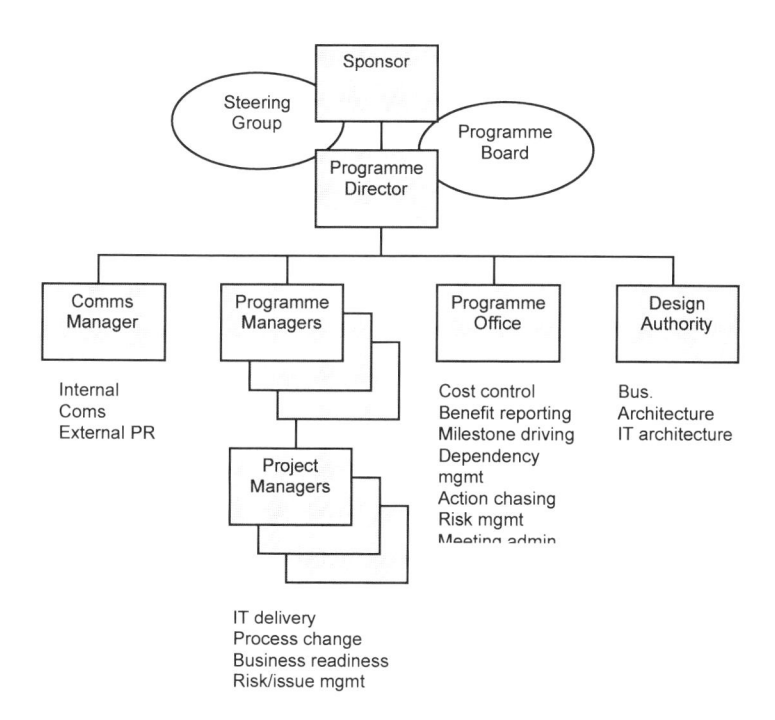

```
                    ┌─────────┐
                    │ Sponsor │
        ┌─────────┐ └────┬────┘
        │Steering │      │      ┌───────────┐
        │ Group   │──────┼──────│ Programme │
        └─────────┘ ┌────┴────┐ │   Board   │
                    │Programme│ └───────────┘
                    │Director │
                    └────┬────┘
```

Comms Manager	Programme Managers	Programme Office	Design Authority
Internal Coms		Cost control	Bus. Architecture
External PR	Project Managers	Benefit reporting	IT architecture
		Milestone driving	
	IT delivery	Dependency mgmt	
	Process change	Action chasing	
	Business readiness	Risk mgmt	
	Risk/issue mgmt	Meeting admin	

Roles

This list is not the only way of structuring a programme and much will be dependant on size and complexity. However, it is the favoured structure of most of the people involved in this book.

Sponsor – get the most senior person possible. Large change programmes cost a lot of money and are high risk. They carry significant tangible and intangible benefits. Ask yourself, and the

CEO, what bigger initiatives exist in the company right now. If the answer is none, then the CEO must be the sponsor. Two key roles of the sponsor are the communication of successes and maintaining the priority of the programme. The sponsor is responsible for strategic direction and vision and championing these at every opportunity. At an overall programme level, the sponsor should monitor the costs and benefits and authorise significant change control of the financials. The sponsor is responsible for the integration of the programme with the overall change portfolio with regard to external influences and their impacts. The sponsor will drive, inspire and motivate teams and give attention to key individuals as guided by the programme director. He or she will make many of the tough decisions, either on policy or isolated decisions with major implications.

Programme director – again, get the most senior person possible, as long as they can afford the time. It is preferable for large change programmes that the programme director is full time, and for transformation programmes it is essential. The programme director is not just a figurehead but needs to be an experienced change management person.

Steering group – the most senior team on the programme is responsible for inputs and outputs that are primarily external to the programme. They must comprise of senior stakeholders, the sponsor and programme director, plus some external presence. The steering group's role is to challenge, ensure the vision is still appropriate and being delivered, and the overall cost and benefits are on track. Their unique contribution is to assess the market implications, external communication messages, and any political or environmental influences. Steering group meetings are typically short and focussed.

Programme board – comprises of decision makers, benefit owners project office and key deliverers. The board monitors progress, high level scope management, cost/benefit management, and risk and issue management.

Project boards - All business areas impacted by change should be represented, along with full time delivery managers. A project board is a subset of the main programme board with a similar role at a lower level of detail.

Project Office – Independent and with authority. The project office is responsible for driving task level dates, detailed cost reporting, change controls, benefit management, and highlighting risk and issues with recommendations.

Reporting

I was told an amusing story by a programme manager who was working in a very hierarchical manufacturing company. The leadership style was very much command and control and there was more than a hint of management by fear. The programme manager was due to give his weekly report to his programme sponsor and it was going to be bad news. He knew the sponsor already had the details from the written report so it was less about reporting and more to do with facing the barrage of abuse he was going to receive. He thought back to school days standing outside the headmaster's office.

The programme manager entered the room and saw the fierce look on the sponsor's face. He was pacing around his desk with the programme status report in his hand. The programme manager had some justified reasons for the slippage and cost overrun but suspected that the sponsor wasn't ready to hear them. Behind the desk was a large window overlooking woods and fields. The programme manager's gaze wandered to the window and he saw a dog playing in the field. The dog had something in his mouth that he was shaking vigorously from left to right. It was a rabbit. The rabbit was kicking its legs and desperately trying to release its neck from the grip of the dog's foaming jaws. The programme manager thought to himself, "right now, I wish I was that rabbit".

An amusing tale, but how sad it is that these relationships exist in businesses today. A programme manager would rather be mauled by a rabid dog than face a meeting with his sponsor. I'd like to think that this is rare in most companies today and that there is more of a supportive environment with a team based culture. Either way, the reporting of programme status needs some real care. It needs to be honest but not alarmist, it needs to be positive but not unrealistic. The communications section of this book (chapter 9) discusses the broader issues of reporting in more detail. Here we focus on reporting within the governance structure of a programme.

Steering group

This is optional and depends largely on the organisation structure and available skills. The programme board (discussed below) is concerned with monitoring, decision-making and risk management at the highest level and owns the overall delivery. The steering group often comprises of senior executives from outside the division or organisation, maybe including non-executive directors. The value of this group is obtained from the challenge of experienced senior people and the focus on impacts external to the programme e.g. business strategy, market conditions, regulatory changes, competitor activity. They could potentially change the scope or focus of the programme if the objectives and business case were no longer valid. The meeting frequency would be less than the programme board.

Programme board

The programme board should deal with high level monitoring and management plus anything that was escalated by a project board. Attendance should be kept to a minimum for a most effective meeting and only one person from each area should attend. All business stakeholders should be represented by someone with total authority. Decisions cannot be reversed outside of the meeting. Programme managers should be invited where appropriate i.e. where specific detail is required to make decisions or where they are to be congratulated formally on a milestone.

Decisions should be made available to the whole programme team in order to inform their actions. The project office is responsible for communicating and monitoring decisions and actions.

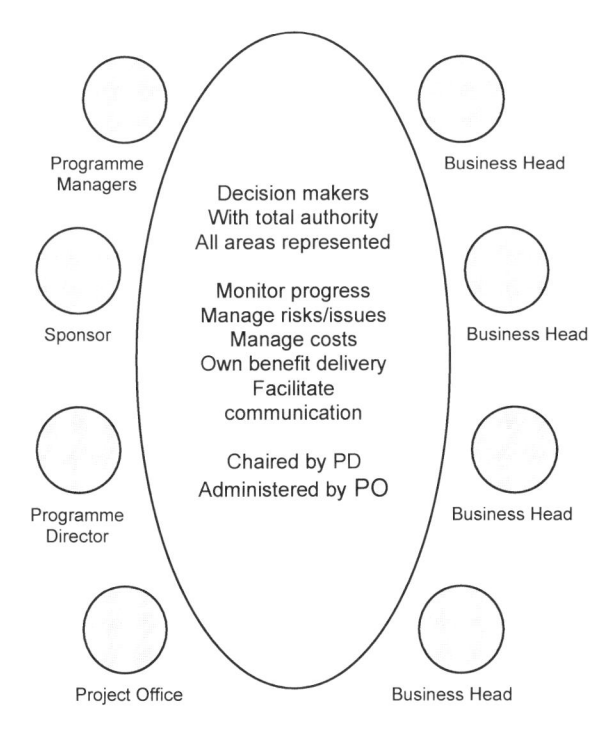

```
        Programme                              Business Head
        Managers        Decision makers
                        With total authority
                        All areas represented

                        Monitor progress
                        Manage risks/issues
        Sponsor         Manage costs          Business Head
                        Own benefit delivery
                        Facilitate
                        communication

                        Chaired by PD
                        Administered by PO
        Programme                              Business Head
        Director


        Project Office                         Business Head
```

Risk Management

In many ways project management and risk management are interchangeable phrases in large programmes. Your methodology will include how to do formal risk management so I'll just highlight some comments that are applicable to everyone, not just the project manager's role.

- Get the balance right and retain a sense of perspective. Alarmist nature of reporting can involve a lot of resource. But don't avoid the risk and let it become a big issue.
- Risk management is a part of everyone's job, particularly the project managers, but also needs someone owning the high level risk log for active management (not just monthly reporting).
- Business risks are also a part of everyone's job. A culture should be created where everyone thinks about the impact of the work they are doing on the customer and shareholder. Business risks should be documented and escalated in the same way as project risks.
- Risk managers and auditors can be useful at all stages of a programme, but are rarely welcome and seen as time wasters. The latter view is true if they are just policing and telling people what they have done wrong. However, they can be valuable if they are being proactive and supportive by highlighting risks early and with mitigating actions.

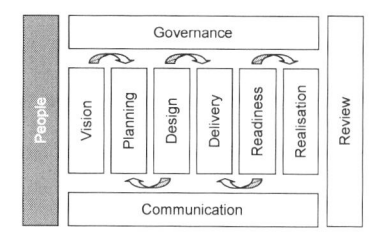

8

People
We do really like change

Topics include:
- Creating teams
- Collaboration versus competition
- Resource management
- Reward & recognition
- The change experience
- The change journey

8: People
We do really like change

Lots of models and tools are developed to cope with the fact that human beings fundamentally don't like change. The experiences of people in this research suggest that they really don't like being 'done to' and need to be involved in the change from vision to implementation. They can then embrace it and enjoy it.

The story below and the first part of this chapter relates to people who are delivering change. The second part is related to people who experience or receive change.

The manager who trusted his team
by a programme manager

The programme was a complex systems migration and we encountered one technical problem after another. The original vision of a clean single architecture for all new and existing business was slowly dissolving. The legacy systems were just too complex and the cost benefit of migration was getting higher and higher. We frequently had battles between the purist architects, the development teams, the benefit manager and the support team. Everyone had their own objectives to achieve and it seemingly was impossible to satisfy them all.

One of the technical projects was way behind schedule and over budget. A decision was required and was escalated to me. There was a choice presented to me by the team who were divided over the recommendation. The first option was to carry on with the current approach and put in a change request to delay the project and seek further funding to complete the project. This option would continue to use the traditional method that had been hugely underestimated. The second choice was an innovative solution that would save money and be quicker than original plan, but was high risk. The technology was new and relatively unproven, as was the supplier (who were also from a different country). The project architects supported the risky option and had done their research, putting forward a compelling case. The fact that the architects were sacrificing the 'clean' single platform solution was a big sign that we were in more trouble with the schedule than I thought. All my experience told me that there were too many unknowns and therefore too many risks for it to be successful. However, the ownership and passion for the solution from the internal team and the suppliers was impressive. The 'traditionalists', however, were resigned to more time and effort and showed little enthusiasm or fight for the cause. I made the decision to take the riskier option because of the attractiveness of the upside and the support of the team.

At first the new technology seemed to be working well and we were gaining time on the project. The suppliers had agreed a fixed price contract so the financial risk was minimal. However, after a few months we hit a block. The technology didn't work for a specific set of circumstances and the team couldn't find a solution. Disaster - we were going to have to go back to the traditional method.

I called a meeting of the project team members who were all waiting for a steer. Do we plough on in the hope of a technical breakthrough or do we count our losses and go back to the proven method? Having taken the risk once, I was pretty sure that going into the room I was going to have to say well done for trying but we will have to go back. The room was silent and at the back were some glum and embarrassed faces, appearing as though they were expecting some reprimand. At the front were some rather smug faces with a 'told you so' look on their faces. The attitudes disappointed me and I gave a small speech to say as much and congratulated the team for trying their best. I then quizzed them further to see if it really was a dead end. Their faces lit up and they re-energised in telling me that they were certain with time that they could find a solution. The other team mocked them. This made the team even more defiant and they gave a rousing speech and commitment to me personally that they wouldn't let me down but they understood the personal risk I would be making and in my position they would find it hard to support continuing. I adjourned the meeting and asked the technical leads to talk me through what they had learned from their failure and what they would do different in approach, technology and resource.

I was satisfied with the reflection, learning and new approach the team were planning. It was not a certainty but their determination and commitment to me was outstanding. Their initial motivation was mainly personal pride and doing the right thing for the business. The motivation now was to reward me for the support I had shown them.

I reconvened the meeting and told them of my reasons for continuing with the riskier option – the benefits, the end game, the new approach, but above all the commitment of the team. A new challenge was now with the traditionalist team who felt they were defeated twice and finding it difficult to stay advocates of the project. I asked for volunteers to join the project team on the basis that we needed more brains to resolve the problem and more resource to make up lost time. Most of them joined with a few exceptions who were moved to a different project, as they were gong to be damaging onlookers. No-one in the new team felt winners or losers because this was a new project, with a new team, combining skills and experience and all with a single goal.

The result was positive and the team found a solution and implemented it within original timescales. The cost was lower due to the fixed price contract and additional support from the supplier at no cost. Everyone won; the team combined and were all heroes. This was recognised as a significant milestone in the programme and motivated other projects to similar levels of commitment.

The personal outcome for me was an overwhelming feeling of pride in the team and satisfaction that a high-risk decision had come off. My leadership reputation had rocketed in the programme and with the board and I was given more trust and faith in future decisions (the next opportunity I had for a similar high risk technical option was not taken!). I had renewed energy to complete the marathon and take on future challenges.

I'm not in a position to discuss the merits of taking the high-risk decision, but there was some clear learning from the experiences of managing the team. The key leadership lessons for me were:

- Role modelling behaviours that you want in others e.g. taking a personal risk for what you believe in.
- Creating a culture that doesn't fear failure but learns from it and has the courage to return to battle armed with new tools and wiser heads.
- Utilising the strength of teams and their commitment. Understanding and leveraging the personal pride and 'hot buttons' for them as individuals and as a group.
- Find a way for everyone to be successful, but ensure the saboteurs are removed.

The first part of this chapter describes some more learning from experiences regarding people who deliver change programmes.

Creating teams

People are going to go through a journey and come out the other side with stories to tell – some epics, some horrors, some comedic and usually some drama. What is certain is that people will not be going through this by themselves. The resource of all large change programmes is made up of teams and the quality of the teams has a direct relationship to the quality of the deliverables. Therefore building high performing teams is one of the critical success factors of a change programme.

> *"I was working long days and nights for months in a Portacabin in a car park with some excellent people. I have not experienced the same excitement and comradery since"*
>
> *systems developer*

As a programme team develops through discovery, analysis, and delivery it will come under stress and in many cases evolve naturally. It may develop natural leaders, team roles, a team personality and some positive bonding. The progress through the *Tuckman* model cycle (forming, storming, norming and performing) will happen naturally over time, but why wait... and can you afford to? There are many team development models and many consultancies that can help build high performing teams. You may have organisational development teams that have a good track record. Whichever solution you use it is important to recognise which teams need which type of development. For example a team who will be together for a year can afford the time to invest in some of the more theoretical models and have the time to reap the benefits of personality types and team roles. Others may be more temporary or fluid and therefore need some short sharp methods and practices. I can say with some confidence that the more you invest in team development the higher they will perform. The best teams can get you out of trouble and perform near miracles. The worst can self-destruct and end in total failure.

As well as team development, there are two best practices that consistently arise in the research from experience of teams in change programmes.

1. Co-location has a massive impact on the performance of cross-functional teams. This is likely to be resisted from a cost and flexibility point of view in onvironments where office space is at a premium. However, there are many benefits that make it worthwhile; in speed and clarity of sharing information, relieving stress, appreciation of others challenges, facilitating joint solution design, and importantly more fun. Some organisations have considered co-location of temporary project teams to be so important that they have re-designed their office space to accommodate transient spaces. With other social and environmental issues effecting location strategies there is more opportunity to include flexible work areas in space planning.

2. Another related factor that is simple to implement is creating the right physical environment for teams who are going to spend a lot of time together. Positive experiences include water fountains, snack facilities, restrooms, play areas, games rooms, fridges, couches, massage chairs, and decor. The important point to note is that people like different things to create their perfect work environment and the best way to found that out is to ask them. When allocating the project space for a new team, treat it like their home for the coming months and allow them to personalise the space. One simple example that worked well in a long programme was to give a small budget to the team to buy some artwork for the walls. They replaced some drab corporate images with bright colours in large shapes. This gave them ownership of the space, extended the time they spent in it, bonded the team in a simple task, and made them feel special.

Collaboration versus Competition

These are two very different strategies to optimise the performance of teams and both have been used extensively. As mentioned before in this book, it is important to have everyone's goals aligned with the business strategy, the programme vision and their own aspirations; everyone pulling together for one aim. But some healthy competition is particularly good for creating a race in order to speed up the delivery.

One example of where I've seen this work well was in a software house where a team's performance influenced which programme or client they worked on in the future. This may have given them opportunities to learn new skills, work with advanced technology, clients with a good brand name, travel to exciting locations, or not travel at all. Providing choice of future projects is a good way of incentivising teams and individuals. Other rewards may include financial, training, holidays or gifts. The essential caveat to instilling competition is that if you can't measure it fairly and transparently then don't do it. If people feel cheated then it will have the opposite effect next time.

> *"Installing a free-vend table football machine in the highest performing team's area showed trust, recognition and brought the team even closer together. Others aspired to be that team"*
>
> *project manager*

Another risk of competition is that if the rewards are so high then it might encourage some teams or individuals to engage in foul play. If winning is so important it is at the expense of others then it is obviously destructive. People may lose sight of the importance of the overall goal. To ensure this always takes priority then winning as an individual or small team can only be rewarded if the larger team achieve the overall programme goals.

Resource Management

Having the right skills to do the right job is a pretty simple concept and certainly easiest at the start of the programme. There is a risk that when there is little pressure at the start, we tend to be more optimistic about our capabilities and the amount of problems we will incur. Skills management throughout the programme needs to be a strong focus. The biggest risks experienced in resource management are:

- **Over reliance on experts**. There will inevitably be an 'A-team' and the rest. The danger is that the A-team are burnt out because of the lack of bench strength in the resource pool. These people need identifying and managing as a separate pool. It is tempting to keep them too long on an assignment or use them too early in the problem management cycle. A percentage of their time needs to be used doing coaching, skills transfer and supervision. Project managers need the discipline not to hold on to the A-team too long. 'Crying wolf' over the need will be damaging for the whole programme and ultimately for their reputation.

- **Under-skilling at design stage**. This is where the experts are critical. You've all seen the graph - if there are errors in the design stage it will cost you much more during subsequent stages than an error later in the project. So it's worth ensuring the architects get it right and the builders can work from the drawings.

- **Overly optimistic resource requirements**. However short you think you are on expertise, you'll be even shorter. I wouldn't advocate blindly over resourcing throughout the programme but work out where the hotspots are likely to be based on complexity, newness, or where the estimates were a bit sketchy. It's more effective to get people up to speed early rather than train them later and distract the experts from critical delivery. Avoid pressure to cut costs at resource planning stage, this is likely to cost more later on.

- **Lack of 'plan B' when under-resourced**. Try for a flexible arrangement with a high calibre agency to call on a pool of quality resources that have been familiarised with the programme. If the PR team have been effective, the competition to supply resources to the programme will be high and therefore some good deals should be available, either on price for known requirements or on flexibility for unknown requirements.

- **Avoidance of external assistance**. Do what you're good at and get help where you have gaps. There is no time for bravado and egotists. This applies to all levels and role types. For example, the use of non-executive directors with similar experience in a different company or sector works well to challenge and provoke thought at the programme board level. Similarly, where there are critical design decisions to be made, seek opinions from experienced people who have been through the same thought process.

- **Acceptance of second best people**. Unless this is another big complex programme in a sequence of many successful similar programmes, programme management is likely to be an area needing help. One or two industry-best people at this level can influence the performance of hundreds beneath them so acquire the right ones. Take up references to ensure they really have done what they said they had. I remember interviewing five people who had single-handedly delivered Britain's first Internet bank! A few top calibre people will make a huge difference compared with an army of mediocre ones.

- **Blinkered focus on today's needs**. Ensure skills transfer is in all plans and in all resource contracts. It is easy to focus on today's resource needs and store up a problem later in the programme or post implementation. Planning for people's next assignment is also important for motivation. An exciting next role can be used as a required for successful delivery and skills development.

- **Inexperienced contract management.** This is a skill in its own right and contracts should be defined and negotiated by someone with experience. They can be obtained from independent consultants or legal firms. They will be expensive but could potentially save a lot of money when things start to deviate from plan, and they will. Contracts should be fixed price or risk/reward where possible. This helps create one team, with skin in the game, and encourages the right behaviour of defining needs clearly at the start (see contract management in the planning chapter).

- **Inexperienced supplier management.** Large numbers of suppliers will require exceptional supplier management skills and clear integrated goals to ensure joined up solutions and deliveries. Supplier management is not always a role in itself but can be a skill required by a programme or project manager who is responsible for the supplier's delivery. There are many techniques that can be learned quickly and these should be in place prior to the resource being assigned to the programme.

- **Failure to recognise the need for a resource manager.** The role of a resource manager is often used in large programmes. They can be used to manage allocation of appropriate people based on changing demand. This will be most successful if a flexible resource pool is in operation. A skills database should be maintained for all programme resources and negotiation with programme and project managers of skill levels and assignment dates. This can be a thankless task where everyone is constantly complaining over the necessary compromises that take place. Therefore a resilient personality is required as well as someone who carries credibility through having had experience of managing and delivering with a programme resource function. The resource manager role also needs to incorporate external consultants and contractors in the resource strategy, supporting the cost manager's targets as well as the skills needs.

Reward & Recognition

This is an area that usually starts off with lots of activity and enthusiasm. Then as the programme becomes more intense the focus drops – which is exactly when it's impact is greatest. Here's some consistent feedback about reward and recognition:

"The pamper hamper sent to my wife with a personal letter from my boss was perfect. She forgave the disturbed holiday and is now more supportive of the hours I work"

operations analyst

- Reward the heroes then try and spread the load to prevent burn out.
- Find out what makes people tick and reward them appropriately. Blanket approaches can work for large numbers but will have less impact than the personal touch. The quote above is a good example for the married man but there are many different people with different lives outside of work. Getting to know your team is a great advantage for any leader who is expecting them to perform heroics.
- Public recognition (internal) can be motivational for individuals and teams but can also be used to point out learning points. If mistakes are made then they should be recognised and highlighted to avoid repetition. One programme used Champagne and gherkins awards on a

regular basis. Champagne was awarded to team members who excelled beyond expectations of them. Gherkins were given to managers who took a wrong decision or gave poor direction. This recognition was in a fun style but made the points well and helped bridge the gap between the leaders and their teams.

Celebrate

Maintaining a 'feel good factor' for the whole team is essential to work on over the period of the programme. Here are some common pieces of feedback about celebration:

- Informal and formal celebrations should be managed at regular intervals and mixed up to stay fresh.
- Key individuals should occasionally have special treatment but all involved should have the opportunity to recognise success and be a part of the winning team.
- Success breeds success and celebration is a way of making people hungry for more and others to look over the fence and want to be included in the party.
- Celebration can be used as a recruitment method for future phases.

I end this part of the people chapter with the most important driver for people working on programmes, which I would categorise as programme advocacy. With the right vision, communication, and understanding of their contribution, most people want to be able to say with enormous pride, "I was a part of that".

The remainder of this chapter deals with people who are experiencing or receiving change.

The change experience

> *"People do like change, they just don't like it being done to them"*

This is a quote from David Firth, an organisational development consultant, who I consider to be a leader in people change. The quote supports a recurring theme in the experiences in this research; that people need to be personally involved in change in order to embrace it.

There are many experiences of tactical or short-term change that are very successful, but over the longer term the changes become less sustainable. This can be down to misaligned systems and processes or inflexible business architecture or IT architecture. But more often than not it is the people receiving the change who gradually reject it. Programme people are rarely concerned with sustainable change as they are not usually around to experience it. They have either gone on to another programme, division, or even company (particularly if they are an external supplier).

There are many versions of the change curve that describe the stages individuals go through before adopting change. The change curve in the picture below is one I've designed to show the typical emotional stages people go through during a change programme.

At the idea stage of a change, many people will feel anxious as they may recall similar changes in the past or simply not know enough about the change to feel comfortable. During the vision stage a certain amount of optimism is felt because this is when all the positive messages are given during launch events, team meetings, and bulletins. One of the real purposes of the vision is to excite people and gain their buy-in at the outset of the change. If people aren't grabbed at this point then it is likely to be a difficult journey, though there are examples where more cynical people are won over later when they see evidence. Then as the planning stage commences, some of the euphoria dies and the details are starting to emerge – high cost, long programme, new ways, different systems, lots to learn, and so on. This causes some fear about the change, which can turn into feeling threatened, as more and more details unfold during the design stage.

What happens next is critical for some people. I have mentioned saboteurs before and they often become active in this stage of the change curve. If during the delivery and implementation stage they don't gradually start to accept the change then it is possible that they become hostile and less passive. I have seen examples when only one or two of these people, depending on their standing among their peers, can be quite destructive and build a following which, at worse, can become mutinous. Some people either can't or won't accept the change and the best course of action for them and others is that they are moved away from it.

As testing progresses and maybe people experience the model office, followed by training, some of the threat caused by unfamiliarity is replaced by gradual acceptance. This increases with experience as people get used to their new role, system, process, or team. Finally, if the benefits have been well signalled, managed and delivered, then people will see evidence of positive change and start having belief in the change. Successful programmes will have a high percentage of advocates at the beginning of a programme and a higher percentage at the end, with a dip in the middle. The management of every individual during the middle stages will contribute a great deal to the success of not only the current programme but also to future changes. The ultimate aim is for an organisation to have a workforce who believes that their change capability is strong and then the change curve will become flatter over time.

Some people will naturally embrace change and some areas will show strong resistance. A number of different methods of taking people on the journey are required. Some key messages from the experience research are:

- Determine where people are on the change curve and follow a different strategy for each group:
    - Reward the advocates and publicly recognise them as role models.
    - Nurture the agnostics and support them.
    - Exit the saboteurs

- Keep the vision alive throughout the programme. During each stage of the programme refer to the key messages that excited people at the outset. Provide evidence that the programme is delivering on elements that provided optimism.

- Involve as many people as possible throughout the programme, not just at the beginning and end. The more people that become familiar with the changes, the less threatened they will feel.

- Ensure the communication is honest. If people start to learn about some negative elements of the change through the back door then their fear will increase and stay for longer.

- Target the influential cynics and, if practical, give them key roles in the change. Turning sceptics into advocates is a powerful demonstration of the benefits of the change to a large population.

The change journey

One inconsistent piece of feedback from the research is the use of professional organisational development functions or consultants. I suspect this is due to who they were and how they were used. I can say that there are definitely success stories and I will describe one that was a piece of innovation under very challenging circumstances.

After an acquisition and then a merger, a new company was formed and wanted to create a compelling vision for its people. The three cultures needed to be brought together with no apparent winners and losers. This was a genuine coming together of three equal parties, all who believed their culture was the best.

The vision was articulated in workshops in a visual way, showing a new world with all its symbols and characteristics. It was aspirational and created a sense of ambition and excitement for the organisation. A good start, but it didn't address the question of "what's in it for me?" This was covered by a programme call 'The Journey'.

The Journey described the aspiration and opportunity for everyone in a way that aligned with the company vision and personalised it to an individual. The first task was to divide the company vision into subjects, each one having its own sub-vision. Again, a strong visual element was used through a map that described a start and end point for every role for each subject. The example map below shows a journey for an analyst role with the subject of team skills.

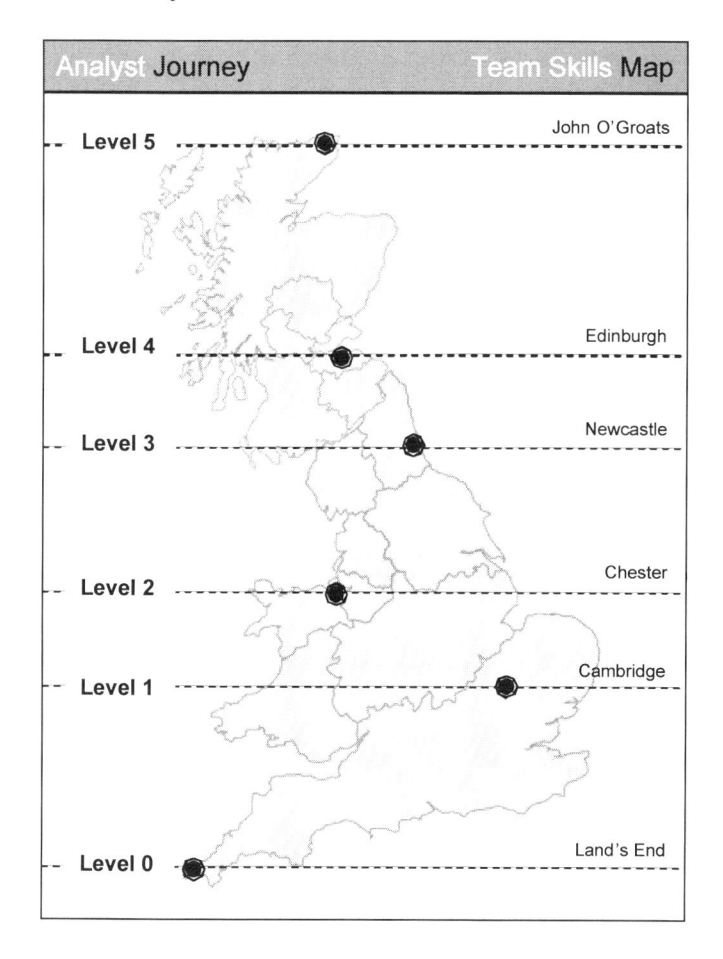

Analyst Journey — Team Skills Map

- Level 5 — John O'Groats
- Level 4 — Edinburgh
- Level 3 — Newcastle
- Level 2 — Chester
- Level 1 — Cambridge
- Level 0 — Land's End

The map shows 5 levels plotted at a point on the map, each having a detailed description of what expectations there were to reach each level. Every person agreed where they were on each of the subject maps and where they wanted to get. Places on maps described competences and skill levels as well as behaviours that supported the cultural vision. Then personal development plans and career plans were agreed so they could progress from place to place.

Most commonly there were 5 places (levels) and 5 maps (subjects). People would plot their own progress on the maps as they develop the required attributes. The Journey complimented existing Human Resources processes with an additional and strong focus on cultural change that was integrated with skills and career development.

The Journey was very successful for the majority of people. It was visual, easy to understand expectations and to monitor progress. It was easy to follow the links from an individual's journey to a team or department one and therefore understanding where people fitted into the big picture. It had aspiration and encouraged thinking of career plans and a broader aspect of personal development and a regular dialogue with people's managers. Above all, it was slowly changing the culture of three departments into one newly formed shared culture (note the word *slowly* - professional organisational development people have told me that 5 years is a realistic timescale for cultural change). But the cultural change journey wasn't successful for everyone because an important part of the journey was missed.

> *"I had never had so much interest shown in me before... not even from my wife!"*
>
> *claims manager*

Some people were resisting the process and although intellectually accepting, were not bought into the change to a new culture. After exploring this further it was apparent that there was a need to help some people leave the past before they could move to the future. They were typically the longer serving colleagues who had the culture engrained in them. They would have been the founders or champions of their culture and had a lot of ownership. They had seen other cultural attempts initiated by various senior managers and they had gone as easily as they started.

This was a different part of the journey and for these people *the change journey starts in the past.* Recognition of this and preparing to invest in going back before going forward was a major step. In order to help people out of the past the champions of the new culture had to go into their worlds with them. Workshops were run that allowed people to describe the past, what was good and bad about it, and what their own roles were. They described the new world and the threats it brought. They then did a series of exercises to connect the two worlds. There were many visual aids and walls were lined with pictures and lots of expressive animation.

If these people could be converted they would be perfect advocates and leaders of the new culture. But if not then it is likely they would be saboteurs and would have no place in the new world.

This approach is a good example of an implementation of elements of a model written by John Kotter and Leonard Shlesinger. They describe six approaches to deal with resistance to change:

1. *Education and Communication.* This was the intellectual element of The Journey and involved communication of the vision.
2. *Participation and Involvement.* This was the co-development of personal maps to support the overall journey.
3. *Facilitation and Support.* This was the delivery of workshops to help people leave the past before embracing the future culture.
4. *Negotiation and Agreement.* On occasions an individual was allowed to change the journey for them self or even have

exceptions (where this would not compromise the overall vision).
5. *Manipulation and Co-option.* Once the resistors were converted, one or two were put in positions of influence, as much for the symbolic nature of their position as for their value.
6. *Explicit and Implicit Coercion.* This was avoided, as there was an exit strategy for saboteurs or those choosing not to join the new world.

Appendix B describes more ways to address resistance to change.

9

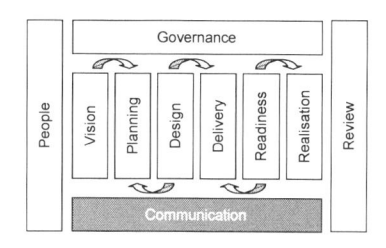

Communication
Shoot the spin doctors

Topics include:
- Balanced messages
- Repetition, repetition, repetition
- Propaganda
- PR pitfalls
- The communication plan
- Stakeholder maps

9: Communication
Shoot the spin doctors

Communication is a critical work stream to help with buy-in, motivation, advocacy, expectation management, and engagement. In many employee opinion or employee morale surveys, communication is a word that is used as an area that often needs improvement. It is also a word that means different things to different people and, in change programmes, this ambiguity can cause teams to believe they are addressing an issue when in fact they are investing in the wrong area. Communications is a profession in its own right and therefore I advocate using the professionals, either internally, externally, or both. It's an area that is often under-valued in change programmes but can be the make or break of a programme in perception or reality.

The killer sentence
by an internal communications executive

The most innovative thing we did on the programme from a communications point of view was the 'day in the life' series. We did some imaginary interviews with real staff based on their future role when the programme would be finished, in 2 years time. First we interviewed them doing their current role and then, based on the programme vision and the changes in the process and systems design, we re-wrote the interview in the future. We had a strong and clear vision for the changes and this was a fabulous way of bringing the vision to life for individuals and answering that all important question of "what does it mean for me?" The interviews were published on the intranet, the in-house magazine, and a special programme bulletin. We even published

168 | Lonely Project

one interview, with a brave customer services agent, on the video magazine that was broadcast to all employees. She projected herself into the future and with all the enthusiasm and excitement she had, delivered a really inspiring performance.

Within a few months we had covered the most common roles and managed to emphasise the key changes over and over again, each time in a different area. The messages were consistent and stayed fresh. This resulted in people looking forward to the changes, as we delivered human content and not just corporate speak or promises about great new systems and processes. We incorporated many other initiatives that were running in parallel to help paint a picture of the future. This included some home working, change to new work-spaces, a new canteen area, multi-skilled work, professional qualifications and a new flexible reward package. Being able to include these cultural changes helped 'sex it up' and take a holistic view of the new world. We all got so bought into it ourselves that we started thinking about entering some competitions for 'best place to work' or 'best communications programme'; the momentum was really building and we were bursting with pride and anticipation.

We chose not to mention that, because of new systems and a lot of process automation, some roles would disappear. We hoped that the current rate of growth and corresponding recruitment would mean that by putting a stop on hiring, new roles could be found for everyone. We didn't see the need to be alarmist at this stage and risk the optimism that was flowing through the organisation.

The whole programme communication strategy was working a treat. As well as the 'tell' type communications of print, video and intranet, we also tried to create as much interaction as possible to really engage our people in the changes. We had Q&A facilities on-line, we had regular climate surveys, and we had some fun polls where people could vote on things that would affect their future working environment. This was very popular as people had the opportunity to influence the smaller but important issues like canteen food, dress code, and parking facilities. We also had 'home movies' where teams could borrow the technology and produce some footage of new products, marketing material, or workshops. Anything that would help keep the vision alive was used to show people what was really happening inside the programme.

All of these facilities required investment and thankfully we had the dedicated resource allocated from both the communications team and the programme. We occasionally used external help if we were short of resource or expertise, but usually we coped well with the existing team. The amount of publicity and 'feel good factor' we generated for the programme and future organisation was fantastic and we had a very happy sponsor. He took a lead role in our communications, but to be honest we made that very easy for him with some excellent scripts, editing and promotion. It was the smallest budget in the whole programme but the investment in communications was proving to be one of the greatest value.

So what went wrong? There was one minor omission that you may have picked up on earlier. It was all good news. Was it really going to be this good? Amazingly, for a historically cynical organisation, we had really captured their imaginations and got a large percentage of believers, evidenced through the anonymous surveys. But we knew there was some uncertainty about future headcount and whether or not there would be job losses. We hoped it wouldn't happen but didn't even signal the possibility. Our board supported the optimistic view and they were enjoying the positive publicity as much as anyone. There was very little challenge as we all got carried away. In hindsight, there needed to be some reality check and some challenge sessions. For example, even if we didn't expect job losses, we knew there would be job changes. How were we going to handle this? Even if they were deemed positive changes, we all know that any change to a persons role needs to be handled with extreme care in order for them to remain motivated.

The first implementation was in a small team and was very much used as a pilot for future changes. It was a success from an implementation and benefit point of view. The automation and process changes worked well and the team gave positive feedback. Some of them would be used on future implementations and others would stay in the team with enhanced roles as per the 'day in the life' series. But for two individuals... just two, and we're talking thousands of people in this organisation... there were no new roles available. They didn't want to be re-trained and didn't want a move to another department. They accepted redundancy. Individually, they were ok with this and in some ways it was their choice. We thought we would be honest about it and put it in the next bulletin. We were clear on the reasons, the choices, the small number and even a quote from one of the individuals, saying that they were happy with the outcome that allowed them to make a complete break. They started a small business and combined a hobby with a profession. It was so positive we even considered doing an article on them.

But it was too late... much too late. In all the months of communication about the change, this was the first mention of job losses or redundancy. The trust was lost in one sentence. People now believed that each implementation was going to come with job losses. They extrapolated forwards and came up with their own numbers of people that were going to change or lose their jobs. These were then being freely discussed as facts. All the focus changed from the positive communications to the negative rumours and the belief was gone. It took months to build and seconds to lose.

As it happened there were only minor numbers of job losses and all of those were volunteers. Slowly the cynics quietened and a level of belief was recaptured among the masses, although never as good as it was at the outset. There was suspicion with every communication in the programme thereafter and even future programmes suffered as they enthusiastically delivered their vision.

The lesson here is obvious and is spelled out by the communications manager. Even when you're unsure, it is better to portray a balanced picture and highlight the risks. Total transparency is unusual in a large organisation and once trust is earned it can be a most powerful tool. The story focuses on the major error but it's worth highlighting some of the really good practices that brought about one of the best pieces of change programme communications I've seen:

- Make it personal. People can intellectually buy in to change visions that focus on the corporate benefits but really want to know the answer to the all-important question of "what's in it for me?"
- Answer that question with honesty and people will respect the programme leadership and believe the positive messages. If its bad, say it is. If there are risks, spell them out clearly. But in every communication, reinforce the positive messages and opportunities for people.
- If you think you've communicated clearly the first time, you're wrong. Different people respond to different types of communication and in different language. Everyone's interested in a different aspect and needs the communication at different times. When you think you've got it right, find ways of repeating the message delivery again and again. It is important to find new ways because pure repetition is a good way of losing people's interest.

- Engage people as much as possible and find ways for them to deliver the communication themselves. Investing time in competitions and other activities where people come up with their own answers is much more powerful than the 'tell' style.
- As well as the professionals, use the strong advocates of the change and especially those who have an influence among the masses. Hearing the messages from the 'real people' is more believable than from the professional communicators.
- Spend what's required on the communications budget and don't try and cut back to save money. It is likely to be the smallest budget in all the programme work streams but one of the critical success factors. Get the people onside and they will forgive you of almost anything. A missing piece of scope or a reduced level of documentation will be far more palatable if you have everyone wanting the changes.

"I suspected propaganda and when the bad news finally came out I knew it had all been spin. They must think we're really stupid"

finance administrator

- Use the leaders and make them very visible in promoting and supporting the changes. They don't have to write their words or scripts but they need to have the visibility. Most organisations are hierarchical and look to the people at the top for re-enforcement.
- Make use of a pilot or any other quick wins to demonstrate reality as soon as possible. People will get bored of hearing the hype and will only really believe when change actually occurs. Use the first change as an opportunity to repeat all the key messages again, but this time as facts.
- Can't say it enough times – be honest about the risk, without being alarmist.

Below are the most common pieces of advice reported in experiences of communications work streams in change programmes from the research. In many cases they are the same as in the story, which is reassuring, and in these instances I've kept it brief. But remember, I've just said that repetition is important to get across the key messages.

- Repetition, repetition, repetition! Use the same messages over and over again – vision, strategy, targets, progress, etc. Most people will not grasp what you are saying until they have heard it many times, from many people and in many different vehicles. Unless you know everyone individually you will not find his or her hotspot the first time.
- Open monitoring. Report progress regularly, simply and refer to the key messages at every opportunity. This not only helps with where you are in the programme but also re-iterates the value of each achievement with regard to the overall objectives. Some achievements need to be targeted at groups who are most interested or involved. Others need to have the information available to them in case they look for it. Even if you believe they wouldn't be interested in the detailed minutes from an individual work stream progress meeting, make it available so they don't think you're hiding anything. It doesn't cost you much to have an intranet site with all the reports on it. This also avoids rumours because there is a single version of the truth available to everyone. Make it searchable for easy access to selected subject matter.

"I don't think I'd ever been so respected as when I went public on a big cock-up we'd made. People started to believe the good stuff after that, without suspicion of spin"

programme director

- Admit your mistakes. It's a great way of getting support. Culturally, we often like the underdog and we want them to succeed. We also tend to want to knock the heroes. The balance is important and can be like walking a tightrope. Too much weight on the mistakes and you lose confidence. Too much weight on the success and people want to knock you down.
- Public recognition. Recognise good performances, people, and outcomes to the whole programme and to other interested areas. This is motivational for the teams and also generates a sense of excitement for those who will be involved later on. But be sensitive to individual preferences. Some people don't like their name in lights and would actually be motivated to fail to avoid re-occurrence. I have found that these are few and far between and even those who say they don't like a fuss do like a small one. Just don't make them do a speech.

"The comms team had an uncanny knack of nipping every rumour in the bud before it grew out of control. It was like they had hidden microphones in the toilets"

IT analyst

- Inspiring. Sex it up and make it *the* programme to work on (not the poisoned challis). Take every opportunity to show how individuals have been rewarded, how competitive advantage has been gained, how big and brave it is in a *Star Trek* mission kind of way. Having said that, a short word of warning about using actual references to films or famous characters – people have different tastes and some can be alienated. One mistake made in a programme was when the sponsor referred to it as a particular football club he supported. A bit naïve as there were many negative jokes being told about the programme and some people not even

wishing to associate with it. Music and sport are the high risk ones as they have so much personal identity, good and bad.
- Honest. Being truthful about bad news gains tremendous credibility. In a world where people are used to more and more spin it is refreshing and builds trust. Without trivialising the key message of the communication it is preferable to include bad news in a 'news sandwich' with the topping and tailing of something positive. This avoids total gloom and doom and leaves a message of context, meaning that it is not a disaster and other elements are progressing well. I have even emphasised some trivial piece of bad news to make the good stuff even more believable. There is often the belief that if something is too good to be true then it probably is. Add in a bit of disappointment and everyone's happy!

"Once I knew that the product was going to be on television, I was proud to be working on the programme. I could say to my friends and family 'I did that' "

project manager

- Professional. Engage experts from communications teams, marketing teams, and consultants. As well as good delivery of communications and branding, the experts will be able to contextualise the messages to fit in with the overall programme vision and other key activities and objectives in the organisation. As important as the programme is, it is not the only thing going on and should not have the impression of being at the expense of everything else. A previous bullet talked of 'sexing it up' and the counter risk to that is elitism and even potential sabotage from those not involved. The language is also something the experts can help with to ensure that programme jargon isn't used and the translation is in the words of the recipients.

- Timing is key. This is important on two levels. Firstly, old news is boring so the programme communication must be early enough that it is received before hearsay. There will always be rumours and that's unavoidable, but as soon as it's ready, push the button. Secondly, the initial communication should be before the programme has even started. The use of initiation events as people are assigned will ensure they are informed right from the outset and this will help with advocacy. As a rule, early communication is best, but if its too early it can be worn out before it becomes relevant. Teaser campaigns are good as long as not too much is communicated such that it has to be retracted or changed once the programme gets underway.

> *"The IT director came to my desk and told me I was doing a great job and I felt 2 feet taller. Then he asked me what I was working on and I felt even less valued"*
>
> IT Developer

- Use authority. Involve the most senior people possible to re-enforce key messages. This is not only for vision, but also for progress and even individual recognition. As much as I wish it wasn't true, most people listen more to those higher up the organisation structure. For example, a pat on the back from the CEO in person can carry as much weight as a gift voucher, and cheaper! It is also important that people in the detail of the programme understand the involvement of the key decision makers and those steering the ship. If the senior people are bothering to get involved then it must mean it's worthwhile and significant.
- Variety. Use every method of communication possible, as everyone is receptive to different communication vehicles. Some like to use an intranet as their primary communication source as they can peruse when it is right for them. Others

prefer face to face and the human touch. Some people are more visual and need diagrams, pictures and video. Using all methods not only accommodates all people's preferences but also ensure the messages are repeated (have I mentioned that before?).

- Individual. High-level vision statements and objectives are important and its essential that people know how the programme is performing as a whole. It is also critical to answer the question "what does this mean to me?" At an individual level this is usually through cascading and interpreting key messages. At a personal level, case studies are a good tool. These could be a day in the life of a developer during the programme or of a user in the new world. Taking an external perspective is a good way of keeping the focus on the customer and how life will be different for them. A positive case study from a customer viewpoint is also a great way of re-enforcing how worthy the programme benefits are in a wider perspective. People are often motivated by being able to talk about their programme relative to what's happening in the outside world. It makes for much more meaningful conversation in the pub or at home.

Public Relations (PR)

PR is a minefield that can be a great help to a programme or cause real problems and therefore should be dealt with by the professionals.

"I was shocked and embarrassed to see my negative comments about our solution in the computing press. I was only making a sarcastic joke"

Systems Architect

A proactive external communication plan isn't always necessary for every type of change as some have very little impact outside the organisation. However, one misguided comment or even a made-up rumour can require a quick defensive response and this must come from a professional.

I remember doing some media training once and was amazed by the new set of skills and language that was required to address the questions of journalists. Thankfully, it is usually only a select few who have the opportunity, or challenge, of speaking with the outside world and representing the organisation. So here is a summary of the few experiences people have had in the PR world.

- If there is an amount of PR happening because of positive external impacts of the change programme (e.g. new product launch) then use it to build a sense of excitement and pride in the programme. By making the publicity well known internally it can help promote the credibility of the programme and attract people to want to be involved.
- Make the PR material available to everyone, before its released if that's feasible. If people are reading about it in the press or trade papers then they will feel good about it internally and when meeting external suppliers. If TV, radio or other advertising is being prepared then show the programme team in advance so they can feel privileged as well as get excited.
- Suppliers and press will be glad to write articles if there's a good story to be told but be warned that bad news often makes for a better story than good news. Use professional PR people to do it and have a strict policy that doesn't allow individuals to talk to external bodies. They may be tricked into saying the wrong things or giving personal opinions about the organisation.
- Good PR will mean that suppliers will want to be associated with the programme and may offer better terms in order to

get a reference on the back of positive publicity. I remember a particularly difficult negotiation with a supplier suddenly going all my way when they found out who we were using for our advertising. They wanted to be associated with the product and person and were giving things away in return for a piece of valuable press coverage and references.
- External communication of programme targets, benefits, scope or dates before or during a programme is a risk. If the programme fails then it is very public. If the risk is considered too high then only post implementation PR should be used, or at least at a time when success is almost certain.
- Assign an external PR person to present messages to the customer, suppliers, intermediaries, regulators, shareholders and partners. These messages are different and need careful language and content in the context of their audience.

Communications plan

I've often heard it said that some of the best communicators are the worst planners. What I think is really meant by that statement is that some of the best deliverers of communication are not the best to plan a communication. We have all seen some amazing on-stage performers in seminars, workshops and conferences. We also know that not all of them write their own scripts. Some do, based on some key messages fed to them by others who have the wider picture, and can ensure that the content of their speech integrates well with other messages. All messages delivered from a programme, whether it be a conference speech or a written progress report, should be integrated. They should be consistent in content and timely in delivery. They should be part of a communication plan.

The communication plan should have the same rigour and detail applied to it as any other plan in the programme. It should be monitored, reported on and constantly revised in line with other plans. It should be owned by the communications work stream manager who is accountable for the delivery of every activity on the plan as well as the overall vision. I often see communications plans in two formats. The first format is defined in the same tool as all other project plans (using Microsoft Project, PMW, or other scheduling tools). This ensures integration can take place at the lowest task level with all the dependencies in place. However, these scheduling tools do not produce good output for communication. The other format is more pictorial, colourful and friendly. It is often in the form of a large-scale calendar with major milestones and significant diary events. The diagram below shows an example of a communications calendar that would be on the walls of the offices. It signals the variety of positive communication that is happening and usually has people looking forward to events and information. The calendar itself is a good way of showing people the level of communication available should they choose to use it.

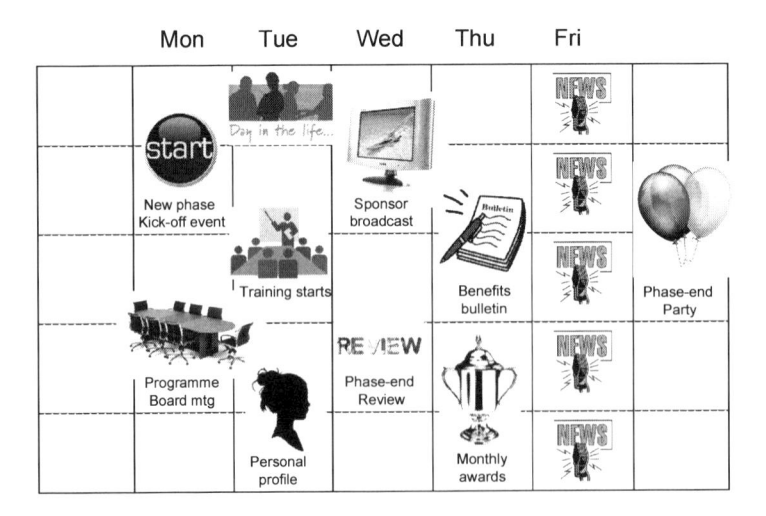

Mon	Tue	Wed	Thu	Fri
start	Day in the life...	Sponsor broadcast		NEWS
New phase Kick-off event	Training starts		Bulletin	NEWS
			Benefits bulletin	NEWS
Programme Board mtg		REVIEW Phase-end Review		Phase-end Party
	Personal profile		Monthly awards	NEWS

The separation of these two plans for two very different purposes is worthwhile in order to meet their individual needs. The risk is that they become detached and then the communication bears no resemblance to what is really being delivered and when. The communication work stream manager must ensure the two are synchronised.

Stakeholder maps

Another useful plan is a stakeholder map where a work stream leader has a diagram of every key individual they need to communicate with. This may be for reporting to or sharing information or receiving updates, it will depend on the role.

Example stakeholder map

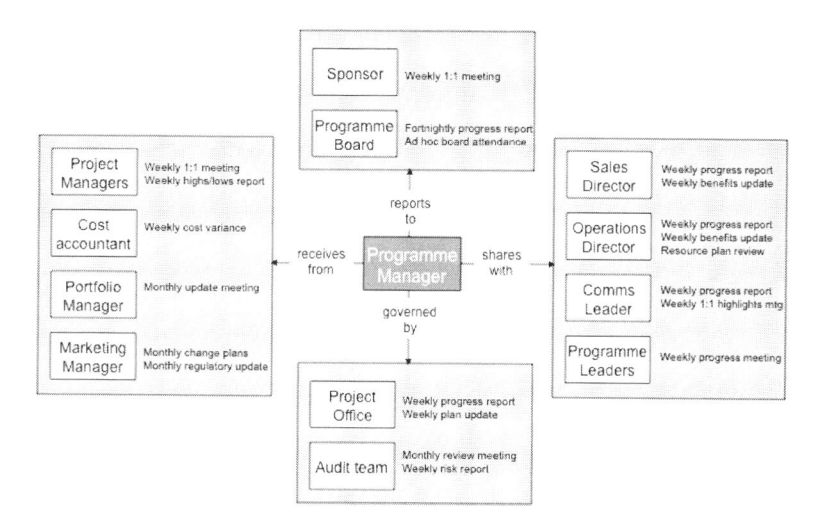

Sponsor	Weekly 1:1 meeting
Programme Board	Fortnightly progress report; Ad hoc board attendance
Project Managers	Weekly 1:1 meeting; Weekly highs/lows report
Cost accountant	Weekly cost variance
Portfolio Manager	Monthly update meeting
Marketing Manager	Monthly change plans; Monthly regulatory update
Sales Director	Weekly progress report; Weekly benefits update
Operations Director	Weekly progress report; Weekly benefits update; Resource plan review
Comms Leader	Weekly progress report; Weekly 1:1 highlights mtg
Programme Leaders	Weekly progress meeting
Project Office	Weekly progress report; Weekly plan update
Audit team	Monthly review meeting; Weekly risk report

The Programme Manager reports to Programme Board, receives from Project Managers/Cost accountant/Portfolio Manager/Marketing Manager, shares with Sales Director/Operations Director/Comms Leader/Programme Leaders, and is governed by Project Office/Audit team.

The personal use is quite obvious and that is a reminder of who to talk to, when and about what. A more important mistake that is made in stakeholder management is over communicating to some people and under communicating to others. It is common for the senior stakeholders to have a queue of people wanting to tell them good news and raise their profile. It is also common for senior stakeholders to be in the dark when it comes to bad news. Both can be equally damaging to the programmes credibility and reputation. If a product manager is told 7 times in one afternoon that the product testing is complete ahead of schedule, he will start to think that the programme is not being managed well. Equally, if nobody tells the finance director about a potential cost overrun until they hear it in the programme board meeting then he or she will become suspicious of the reporting and the risk management.

A stakeholder map like the one above is a fairly simple diagram to draw, but it is quite a challenge to layer a number of them on each other and discover the areas of over or under communication. This can be a role undertaken by the programme office or administration area. A database tool is a good way of being able to identify high and low numbers as a starting point. In addition, there needs to be a level of intelligence applied to this data based on timing, frequency, and content. Like any plan, the stakeholder map needs to be interpreted and maintained. If it just becomes an administrative overhead then it is not only useless but is costing time, money and management diversion.

"I was the most popular person in the world when there was good news to be told but no-one stepped forward when the tough messages needed delivering"

operations director

Typically a stakeholder map database would include the following data elements:

- Communicator – the programme person owning the communication.
- Stakeholder name and role – the person receiving the communication.
- Content – the information to be shared.
- Frequency – how often the information is shared.
- Format – what medium the content is delivered in.
- Alternative communicator – person delegated to deliver in exceptional circumstances.

From this, simple reports can be run to ensure there isn't under or over communication of versions of content to stakeholders. There is a risk of following a stakeholder map too precisely and common sense should be applied. It is also important to retain a human element to communication and avoid a robotic approach. The IT director who did the rounds at 3pm every Friday often had old news or no news to communicate and although his intentions were good, people stopped listening.

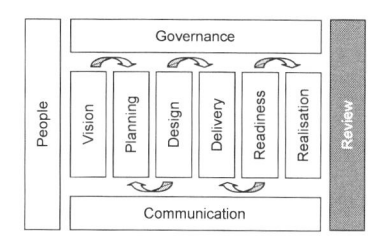

10

Review
What went right

Topics include:
- Why do a review?
- Continuous improvement
- Learning from failure
- Review results
- Phase end review
- Post implementation review

10: Review
What went right

I thought about titling this book 'The Ultimate PIR' (post implementation review). It's full of learning from experience and determining what went right and what went wrong. It has produced some good and bad practice based on real life examples and introduced the occasional theory. I have found it an incredibly useful exercise and am now a convert of the review process as a tool to be used before, during and after change programmes.

And then I got fired
by a programme office manager

I feel cheated, hard done by, and yet quite glad of what happened to me. The experience was definitely full of ups and downs but the learning for me personally has set me up well for my future career.

My task was to establish a new programme office with a new set of tools and processes, new people, and with new investment. It was recognised that previous programme offices were just reporting mechanisms and were regarded as irritating admin functions. The governance element was reasonably well established and just needed a bit more authority and voice. I brought in a couple of people I'd worked with before and they quickly set up new benefit management and cost management processes and tools. Templates were provided and a website was built. This was welcomed as it was seen as good support for an important and previously neglected activity the project managers needed to do. The really big change, and one that was most resisted at first, was the introduction of formal reviews.

Reviews were only done once, at the end of the programme. They were badly attended and poorly facilitated. The outputs were lists that were filed away as part of the programme documentation. The behaviours in the review meetings were accusing and defensive. Although there wasn't a particularly strong blame culture in the company, there certainly was one in the PIR. Any cross-functional team bonding that was built during the programme was often destroyed in the PIR. I was fairly confident I could change this in the same way the cost and benefit management processes and tools helped the project managers. Wrong!

My first tactic was to re-brand the reviews and call them 'learning events'. That clearly signalled them as a positive experience with the focus on improvement. Unfortunately this was tarred with the same brush as the previously implemented learning and development manual – a consultant-led bureaucratic bunch of forms that added little value. Of course they were really nothing of the sort. The focus was all about reflection and learning to avoid making similar mistakes in the future. In fact it was not even driven by mistakes but a large part of the process was what went right and how we can inform future programmes to encourage use of best practice. This was seen as back-slapping for managers to show how good they were to their boss. I persevered regardless of the feedback as I had built some credibility for other new processes and tools and because I was convinced that once they were practiced, people would see the value of the reviews.

Reviews were implemented at all stages of the programme. At first we'd look at similar programmes in our database to see what we can learn before we start. As there wasn't any valuable data at this point we used peoples memories. Not ideal but good for engagement and acknowledgement of experience and skills. Then we did phase-end reviews, peer reviews of every deliverable (e.g. test pans, design documents, training modules, code walkthroughs), and of course the post-implementation review. We were accumulating a lot of data and had a full time person inputting to a database and providing an intelligent catalogue and search facility. Adherence to the new processes was good as I had senior management sponsorship. The data was building nicely and the review skills were being developed. We had new roles (not full time jobs) such as facilitator and scribe. Above all, there was a growing culture of positive learning rather than negative behaviour. I was really pleased with the progress and was convinced I was building the ultimate learning process that would have a huge impact on our programme capability and results.

Then I got fired.

Well, not exactly fired, but asked to do something different. There was a concern over costs and all overhead functions were under scrutiny. We had invested a lot and not only built a new programme office but introduced new roles in projects that were an additional cost in terms of time. But nobody would consider the benefits. We hadn't been going long enough for the increased productivity and effectiveness of programme delivery to materialise. It was very short sighted and hugely disappointing on behalf of my sponsor. Intellectually they could see that this was probably the single biggest thing that would reduce programme costs in the future. But they needed cost reduction now. I had a growing database of learning from all sorts of change programmes. Sadly, no-one ever referred to it and no-one ever learned from it.

On reflection, and having conducted my own review of this experience, I should have made a more direct link to the learning data with the improved estimates and performance of programmes. I should also have got some advocates to be more vocal when they had used some best practice from a review. I should have engaged with the communications team to help market the successes.

I didn't accept the offer of a new role and am now a consultant in setting up and improving programme offices. It would have been sacrilege to not use all that learning!

It's a familiar story where, in an attempt to save money, one of the areas that is reduced or eliminated is one of the areas that can help the most. The review process, if performed well, can save money and time and increase quality, not only for current programmes but for future ones too.

In the story there are many good practices that were adopted and a few improvements that could have been made:

Best practice

- There was strong sponsorship (at first) from the programme sponsor and senior management. This allowed the project office time and money to establish itself and gave them the authority to obtain adherence to its processes.
- It was recognised that project offices don't add value if they are just reporting mechanisms. They need to shift from 'irritating admin' to being perceived as enabling the project managers to succeed.
- Tools and process need to be easy to use, concise in data and time demands and accessible on the intranet as well as in print.
- Behaviours in reviews are critical to their success. A charter can be written and posted on the walls to ensure the right behaviours are adopted.
- When reviews are labelled as learning events it removes any negative connotations. They need to be planned,

- facilitated and documented. The focus should be on key learning and not be drowned by trivial pedantic points.
- The focus of a review is on what went right as well as what went wrong. Reviews should always start and end with positives.
- Giving awards in reviews will improve attendance and keep the focus on the positive learning.
- Keep a fully functional learning database from all phases and all programmes. Make this searchable and common in language so that it is usable. Monitor its use and reward learning from prior experience.
- Market the successes of learning. Make direct links between changes in the programme activities and behaviours learned from the reviews, and the improved performance of the programme.

"The PIR is where the witch-hunt starts. We also know it as the post mortem or search for a scapegoat."

technical lead analyst

Worst practice

- A project office with no authority that just provides administrative support and nags for reports by the project managers will eventually fail. These types of project offices are usually populated with underperformers.
- Negative behaviours produce negative results. A blame culture can creep into a review where people are accusing and defensive. This ruins team morale and destroys the trust required for future teamwork.
- Do not allow the project office to be perceived as an overhead. Constantly seek to demonstrate its value.

Continuous improvement

I find it astonishing how many change programmes in this research didn't conduct a formal review at regular intervals during the programme. Consider motor racing where the review, learn and adjust process is extreme. The monitoring of the product (the car and driver during the race) is continuous and adjustments are made throughout the race to improve the chances of winning. This may be a change to pit stop strategy, tyre usage, or minor remote electronic adjustments. So why don't we do continual reviews and adjustments from learning during a change programme. Here are some of the reasons given:

- We didn't have time as we were behind schedule.
- We couldn't get the right people to attend, as they were busy on the next stage.
- It's not in our process to do reviews during a programme.
- It would have been too depressing.
- We don't have a blame culture here.

From these few comments it is clear that the benefit of reflecting on failure, or even success, is not seen as a productive use of time, until the race is over.

Turning every failure into a learning point

In his book *Keep Walking* (co-authored with Dr Richard Hale), Alan Chambers describes the concept of successful failure when referring to a North Polar expedition that didn't achieve its objectives. Alan says that every failure can become a learning point providing you reflect on it and act differently in the future. He analysed his failed expedition in minute detail and documented every learning point to improve his chances of success on his next expedition (which was a great success).

Alan's planning for his next attempt was meticulous and he made improvements to every single aspect of the journey; clothing, food, tools, fitness, mental preparation, and team selection. Despite mitigation against all known risks, still things went different to plan and new obstacles and challenges were presented to the team. At the end of each day they had a review. They reflected, learned and adjusted for the remainder of the journey. If they had left this to the end it would have been another failed attempt and another set of learning for the next one.

Change programmes are no different to polar expeditions in this respect. We must continually reflect and learn in order to change our course of action during the journey and increase our chances of success.

Review results

The experience from the research tells us that the issues most often arising from reviews are:

- The scope of the programme wasn't managed well, most commonly being scope creep without any impact analysis.
- Resource management wasn't sufficient. Many problems were attributed to resources allocated with the wrong skill set or simply not enough resource. This was less common when a resource management function existed, either within the project office or a key resource supplier, such as IT.
- Cost and time estimates were frequently highlighted as the cause of overrun. This was mainly due to them not being revised, as more detailed requirements and design were understood. It was often considered that expectations of estimation accuracy was either not briefed or accepted.
- Benefits were not delivered because benefits were not measured. A consistent weak area in many programmes. At worst, benefits were not defined and at best they were not managed until the end of the programme. Then it was expected that they would be delivered as defined, without any continuous alignment with programme changes throughout the cycle.

- There was usually confusion at some stage of the programme with regard to the vision or strategy. This was either down to poor alignment of programme goals with personal relevance or lack of updating over a long period when the strategy had changed.

The phase end review (PER)

Having established that this is a worthy activity, what is the right way to conduct a PER? In all the different meetings I've attended and documents I've read I would say that there is no single right way to do it as long as the learning points are embedded back in the change management process. Having said that, I do believe there is some best practice that describes a simple 3-stage process for a review. The data collected, the forms used, and the workshops design may all be different depending on the size and complexity of the programme as well as the company culture. The diagram below shows an effective process.

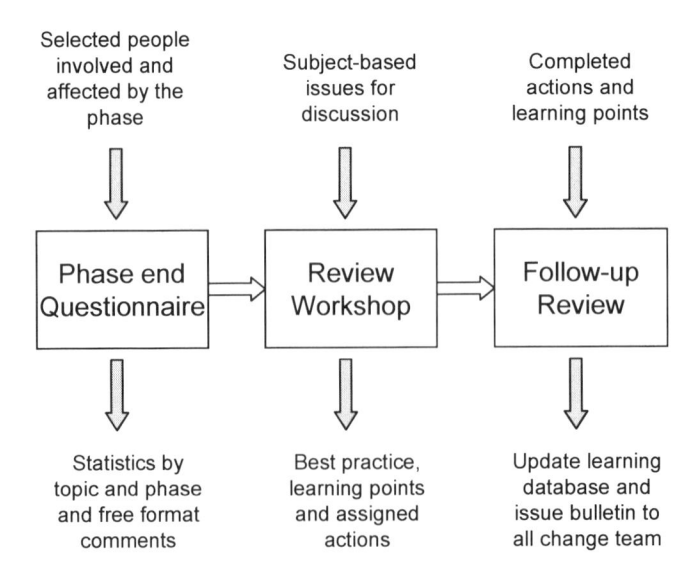

Selected people involved and affected by the phase	Subject-based issues for discussion	Completed actions and learning points
⬇	⬇	⬇
Phase end Questionnaire →	**Review Workshop** →	**Follow-up Review**
⬇	⬇	⬇
Statistics by topic and phase and free format comments	Best practice, learning points and assigned actions	Update learning database and issue bulletin to all change team

Stage 1 - Questionnaire

The issuing of a questionnaire to selected people is a good way of allowing people to answer honestly and anonymously without fear of being accused of apportioning blame. As with all questionnaires, it should be quick and easy to complete or people won't bother. A cross section of people should be used including those directly involved in delivering the programme and those impacted by it. The external input is important to ensure there isn't an insular view of the world and the customer isn't excluded. The number of questionnaires being issued is not that critical providing there is a balance of representation from all disciplines. This ensures the statistics that are used to prepare for the workshop are not skewed. The free format area in the questionnaire is the most valuable. It allows people to comment on their real issues, unprompted by multiple-choice answers to someone else's chosen subject.

Stage 2 – Workshop

A good way of describing the review workshop would be to follow a typical agenda:

1. Objectives. A facilitator needs to be appointed and should be from outside the programme, showing total objectivity. They should also be an experienced facilitator, who often comes from the project office. The first task is to set the objectives for the meeting and talk through the meeting rules. Both should be posted on the walls so that they can be referred to if the meeting strays from the objectives or behaviours become inappropriate. A good starting point for a set of meeting guidelines is documented in appendix G.

2. Introduction. The attendees will be from a broad range of functions, skills and seniority and therefore it is unlikely that everyone will know each other. They are also split into teams that are deliberately cross-functional in order to get a balanced debate during the team exercise. So introductions

are necessary. These can be just a quick round table roll call of name and role in the programme or it can be in the form of an ice-breaker or game. These can be very effective but also very samey. If people are used to the same old games then they will be turned off immediately. Also, if it goes on for too long they will lose the point of the exercise and it become bigger than the workshop itself. If you do an ice-breaker, make it short and keep it fresh.

3. Feedback. The facilitator or project/programme manager presents the feedback from the questionnaire, firstly the statistics and then the trends form the narrative section. This gives the attendees a good flavour of what went right and what needs improving. The subject areas are then introduced and one assigned to each table.

4. Team analysis. Each team works on the subject and considers the good practice that should be taken forward for future phases. They then identify the issues for resolving or improving. Typically, this is the easier bit as people often find it more natural to be critical than give praise, especially of themselves. A leader of a team is pre-assigned and it is their responsibility to ensure that the meeting behaviours are adhered to and that the outputs are produced in the time frame. The sessions are kept short; say 20 minutes, so that everyone is kept focussed. If the environment is right then all the good stuff should come out early. The team leader is also assigned as the presenter back to the group so that there is no fear amongst the group and they can focus on the debate. Finally, recommended actions are documented but not assigned. It is important for the group to concentrate on what needs doing before deciding who needs to do it.

5. Presentation. The team leaders then present back in plenary and after group debate, revise their work. This is facilitated such that everyone gets a say and all the points are

captured. Again, presentations should be short in order to retain energy and flow. It is likely that there are more subject areas than teams and so the process is repeated until all subjects are covered.

6. Summary. During a break, the facilitators prepare the summary of positive learning and the actions to address the issues. Actions are then assigned to attendees. Its important to get buy-in here as reluctant acceptance of actions normally means they don't get done. Be aggressive on timescales because the outputs are required for the next phases of the programme. Larger and longer term actions should be managed by the project office and assigned to the appropriate department.

7. Awards. There's a chance that people are now feeling a bit jaded and even depressed at the amount of work needed to address mounting number of areas to improve for future phases. So, to end on a high and remind people of the good learning experiences, it is time to hand out some awards. This could be for anything an individual or team has done to enhance the programmes likelihood of success. It could be tangible deliverables or behavioural, either way it must be motivational for the recipients and observers.

Stage 3 – Follow-up Review

If the monitoring of actions has been productive then the meeting should be short and efficient. People responsible for actions should be present and confirm their actions completed. If there is minimal debate required then this could be a conference call. The project office can then ensure that the best practice and the improvements made are embedded in the remaining phases of the programme. The learning database should be updated and a bulletin sent to all the change management community with a link to the database, highlighting the key learning. That, to me, is a good review.

My own experience is that a PER is only valuable if the right people attend with the right attitude. The behaviours can be role modelled by senior attendees and controlled by an experienced facilitator. There should be a scribe from the project office who collates key learning for future projects and, usually, project managers who take actions to make adjustments as agreed. Agreement and buy-in to changes is essential so that people leave the event motivated to succeed and with a feeling of enhanced knowledge and experience.

The post implementation review (PIR)

The concept of the PER is reasonably easy to buy-in to; it's to improve the chances of success and achieving the programme team's goals. The PIR at the end is not so easy to convince people of its value because success or failure has already been decided. The team has often already disbanded before the PIR process begins and people are now focussed on new challenges.

Many people's experience of a PIR is not a good one. Attendees arrive defensive, looking at all the things that went wrong, trying to find someone else to blame to take the heat off of them. The PIR can be very destructive, ruin any team spirit that has been hard earned, and give an overall feeling of failure. That's why the focus needs to be on success and what went right, as well as what could have gone better. The process is very similar to the PER but covering the entire programme. It is an accumulation of all the PER data and a review of what learning was actually implemented. The focus is on what can be learned for future programmes as well as for individual skill and knowledge.

We all know that you can learn invaluable lessons from mistakes, but also sharing positive results and successes can be a learning experience for many others.

This whole book is about learning from others experience and personally I think there is no better way of surviving and thriving in the challenging world of change management.

Appendices

Appendix A

10 mildly interesting statistics

Appendix A
10 mildly interesting statistics

Here's a list of some of the most interesting statistics compiled from the research, generated from interviews and questionnaires.

I'm not a massive fan of raw statistics like these, as they are not written with any context. I'll let you draw your own conclusions, but one thing is without question; there is room for improvement in the success rate of large and complex change programmes.

1. 21% of projects were cancelled before completion. More were cancelled towards the end of the project cycle than at the beginning.

2. 88% of projects exceeded deadline, budget, or both. The larger the project, the larger the overrun.

3. Average cost overruns were 45%.

4. Average time overruns were 32%.

5. Large programmes delivered 62% of the original scope. Small programmes delivered 83%.

6. 48% of people believed they had an effective programme management office in place. Less than half thought the reporting was useful.

7. 74% of projects were successful in the eyes of the management, 61% deemed successful by programme teams, and 52% by programme customers.

8. 36% of people did not understand how the programme improved their business, failing the 'was it worth it?' question.

9. 40% of the projects failed to demonstrate that they achieved their business case within one year of going live, and realisation took on average 6 months longer than expected.

10. Support costs were an average of 20% higher than plan for the year following implementation.

Appendix B

10 ways to tackle change resistance

Appendix B
10 ways to tackle change resistance

Many of us have been in meetings or in front of audiences where we've tried to address some resistance to a change. This is usually because the communication work stream has not been effective enough. In a recovery situation, here are some ways of addressing the resistance and gaining support for the change. Face to face is the best way to do this, so that it is personal and can facilitate questions.

1. **Demonstrate buy-in from others.**

    If peers and bosses are supporting the change then it will be more difficult to be a lone detractor. Bring them in to the meeting and ask them to actively support the change from their point of view. Personal situations are the most powerful.

2. **Provide case studies of similar changes.**

    Proven solutions and successful examples will provide credibility to the change. The closer to home they are the better, or if with external companies then the bigger the names the better. Competitor studies are also good because not doing the change should imply that competitive advantage would be lost.

3. **Show alignment to company strategy.**

    If the change supports several strategic goals then it is likely to be more aligned than some existing changes. This is another way of demonstrating senior management buy-in, as everyone should have heard about the strategy and objectives as being critical to the organisations success. Aligning to other changes in the portfolio is also effective, particularly if the resistors are involved in the programmes.

4. **Show personal benefits to individuals.**

   Prepare some answers to the question "what's in it for me?' by generic role and for specific people in the audience. This is the most powerful way of gaining buy-in, but does hold some risk. If you get it wrong and don't hit the right buttons, through not knowing an individual, then the opposite impact could be made. Do your homework on this one or don't attempt it.

5. **Show how success will be measured.**

   Use existing measures that people relate to and produce graphs to show visual improvements. This should show how the changes would make them more successful by using their own performance indicators.

6. **Show the engagement of learning & development teams.**

   One of the great motivators for people, usually above financial reward, is developing their skills, market value and career opportunities. Most changes will require some training, coaching or some aspect of learning. Using the professionals to communicate this will imply that the changes are significant and will help develop people.

7. **Show how it will benefit all stakeholders.**

   If there is a good balance between the benefit to customers, shareholders and employees then there can be little practical challenge to the benefits. Show this visually and summarise how everyone benefits, as evenly as possible. That way it can't be labelled as a cost change or a sales change or anything with previously held negative connotations.

8. Show cultural fit as well as cultural change.

Be honest about the changes but also demonstrate how the change fits with existing values. It is important that people see the change as evolution and that everything they have previously believed in is not being thrown away, forgotten and devalued.

9. Simple communication of the practicalities.

Too much information on the practical elements of the change will bore people and too little will make them nervous. Summarise all the aspects of the implementation to show every area has been thought about. Promise the detail later.

10. Make it personal.

As the leader, say why it is important to you. The more open you can be, the more belief people will have in you and the more following you will get. Sometimes the path to least resistance is from loyalty to the leader.

Appendix C

10 reasons why I failed

Appendix C
10 reasons why I failed

We can often learn more from failure than from success. Certainly in programme management it is not enough to repeat the practices of a successful programme, as every programme is different and requires a combination of new and old thinking. It always amazes me how many times we make the same mistakes and re-learn the lessons of previous experience. This appendix aims to remind us of some of the reasons for failure and hopefully will help prevent repeating old mistakes.

"Why I failed" by a selection of programme managers:

1. I didn't manage the scope and kept agreeing to add more function and keep the end date the same. Each one made a lot of sense in its own right but it soon added up to an impossible task that I was too afraid to admit to... and then I was found out. The extra time and cost were easy to demonstrate but the additional benefits were nowhere to be found.

2. I agreed to the developers' wishes to design a new solution from scratch. The users were happy, the developers were happy and the stakeholders were happy; everybody was going to get what they wanted. After many delays I finally pulled the plug and implemented the vanilla package solution. We overspent, drifted for months beyond the target date and no-one was happy.

3. I pushed them too hard. Whenever the going got tough I didn't make the tough decisions – de-scope, re-phase, own up to the stakeholders early. Instead I made people work

harder and longer. They kept delivering and so I kept demanding. For the one last big push they couldn't respond. We had sickness, emotional problems, team divisions and mutiny. There were so many mistakes uncovered and short cuts taken that it took months to recover. The lack of quality cost us badly.

4. It's easy to call it lack of honesty but I think I convinced myself it was going to be ok. I stopped listening to the team and reported optimistic views to the board with supreme confidence. Had I'd been more in touch with reality they could have helped and the big shock wouldn't have happened. It meant cancelling the programme and re-configuring in smaller projects to hit the minimal scope in time for market launch and regulatory changes. We never gained the competitive advantage promised by the programme at inception.

5. I named the project after my ex-boyfriend. My husband got to hear about it and was suspicious. Jokes were flying around all over the place and in the end I had to pick between the project name and my marriage. It may appear trivial, but renaming the project lost momentum and caused people to think they had underperformed. In fact we delivered the business case but the emotional attachment to the name was lost and the perception was one of failure.

6. I thought the wait to get the requirements finally signed off was going to delay us and was just being bureaucratic. Little did I know that the stalling was due to a fundamental re-think of the product design. We delivered to specification and it went like clockwork throughout the cycle. However, what we delivered was of little use to the business and no-one owned it except me. We did it all over again with less than 50% re-use.

7. It was such a long programme that many people lost interest. At first it was the sexiest thing to work on and then it got tired. The sponsor stop attending meetings and the priority of the programme went from number 1 to also-ran. The good people were moved on to something new and the decision makers went AWOL. In hindsight it was no surprise that it faded away and never completed. The write-off was hidden by a sheepish finance director.

8. Why on earth did we need to outsource? We had a great team with excellent skills. We could apply ourselves to anything, no matter how new it was. Except for this - we lost sight of where our core competences were and ended up bringing in the cavalry. They cost more money than had we engaged with them early and we suffered huge embarrassment watching them take over. The final deliverable was good, but expensive, and the programme was considered an internal failure.

9. It wasn't until mid delivery that I found out that every estimate was optimistic, because there was internal competition for work and the threat of consultancies doing this quicker and cheaper. We had no chance of hitting cost and date targets and, because of re-planning being magnitudes greater than original plan, many of the programme benefits were now unjustifiable. The programme ended up being re-configured into minimalist modules of delivery and was always known as a failure. I should have considered the motives behind the estimates and challenged them rather than just accepting good news so readily.

10. Interesting that I was one of the few people who thought I'd failed (or knew I had). I was so wrapped up in the detail of delivery that I lost sight of the business case. I had a pumped up team who met all the milestones, I was communicating well and reporting lots of good news. I was recognising good

performances and managing risks very early. We delivered on time, full scope and to budget – perfect. Or so it seemed until I reviewed the business case at the end of the programme (for first time since it was written). The design had missed its original objective and no-one had been managing the benefits. Other business events happened that meant this was never noticed. I got away with it… this time.

Appendix D

10 reasons to worry

Appendix D
10 reasons to worry

A good programme manager, sponsor and programme office (with teeth) should constantly be assessing the relevance of a programme. Here are some situations when programmes should be re-visited, re-configured and possibly cancelled.

1. Vision has changed

This probably means the objectives have changed, which means the business case is no longer relevant and the design needs changing, which means the plan is no longer relevant. So you need a new programme that starts from the initiation again. You should look for re-use opportunities to minimise the write-off.

2. Scope is out of control and unachievable.

This means the benefits defined in the business case will not be achieved. The programme either needs cancelling and re-starting from initiation, or re-configuring the essential scope into smaller projects with a new plan.

3. Cost forecast exceeds plan

If the predicted costs are going to exceed the maximum acceptable level to deliver the required return on investment then a revisit of scope and plan is required. Either the programme needs cancelling or re-configuring to eliminate all but the highest value deliverables at the lowest cost.

4. Strategy has changed

It is likely that, with a different business strategy, that the long-term benefits are no longer there. If so, then the programme either needs to be cancelled or re-configured to deliver only short-term payback scope.

5. The design doesn't work

A typical response to this, after so much investment and time at this stage is to make it fit. This is rarely the right decision and causes problems later in delivery and particularly readiness and realisation. If a new solution cannot be found then the programme should be cancelled. At the very least, the programme plan needs revisiting and therefore the ROI will change. If this still doesn't work, then the programme should be cancelled and the write-off accepted. It will be a larger write-off later in the programme.

6. Benefits are no longer realistic

This is a hard one to admit to and often an easy one to fudge. If new benefits can't be found then the business case needs revisiting, which means a review of scope, design, and the plan. If the required ROI still can't be achieved in a re-configured programme then cancel as early as possible to avoid larger write-off.

7. Reporting is inaccurate or has stopped.

A sure sign of a programme that is out of control is one where reporting has conflicting data or is at odds with verbal updates. Alarm bells should definitely be ringing if it has stopped altogether. The programme should be temporarily put on hold and hopefully the right controls put back in place. It is likely the reporting is in a mess for a reason and it is also likely it's one of the other reasons in this list and requires action.

8. The sponsor has gone AWOL

This may be a small problem or a big problem. If the sponsor is no longer interested in the programme then it is likely to be significant. Maybe the strategy has changed or maybe the business benefits are no longer relevant. Either way, the cause of change in interest needs to be understood. If the sponsor is still interested but no longer active, then this is less of an immediate problem but ultimately may need a change in sponsor. Without strong leadership, a programme is likely to dwindle and fail.

9. The programme team are fighting

It may seem pretty obvious that this is an indication of a problem, but many programme managers gloss over it as stress related due to the pressures of hard work. However, it is usually more deep-rooted than that and a sign that handovers between stages will not meet gateway criteria. This means there is an increasing likelihood that the end product will not deliver against plan or quality. It's important to address the squabbles in both group and individual sessions. The time will be a sensible investment and a part of good risk management.

10. The suppliers are breeding

If you see an unexpected growing number of consultants and external suppliers in the building then one of two things are probably happening. You are being fleeced or you are way behind plan. If they are on a time and materials contract then your costs are likely to go up as a result of trying to recover time against plan. If you are on a fixed base contract then there is either a time or quality problem they are trying to recover. Without openness and agreement on the way forward, the end result is likely to be poor quality from cut corners and ultimately a cost overrun due to delay or re-work. Ensure the reporting is accurate and the relationship is built on trust with a few key individuals.

Of course there are many more signs of issues to worry about whilst managing a change programme and your methodology should include rigorous risk management to identify and assess them.

Appendix E

10 ways to kill an idea

Appendix E
10 ways to kill an idea

At first glance this may not appear to be the most constructive of lists to include in the book, but it can be very helpful to know how some people may be trying to stop a change before it is started. This could be an entire project itself, at the idea stage, or it could be a piece of innovation that gets you out of trouble. Ideas will be thrown around throughout a change programme and without them we would blindly follow processes and methods without improvement. Innovation can be your friend or enemy and not all ideas are good ones or appropriate. In some situations have used detailed analysis to make decisions about ideas and in others I have just gone with them based on intuition. The risk versus reward of every idea needs to be assessed but in the appropriate manner for the specific need.

Here's a list of how people might challenge an idea and therefore you can prepare answers or tactics in advance.

1. Ask for a wider input.

    Requesting more and more people to be involved and putting the idea to the vote will inevitably kill the idea. This tactic shows an apparent support for the idea but is ensuring that process and bureaucracy puts many obstacles in its way. It is likely that even the most enthusiastic of proposers gets worn down and gives up.

2. Ask for case studies

    Evidence is a powerful support for an idea. To the contrary, most initial ideas won't have any internal or external research and need to be developed once given initial support.

Highlighting the lack of evidence and the high risk will reduce the confidence in an idea. If it is pointed out that the idea hasn't been tried before then this raises concerns about the risk.

3. Show how similar ideas have failed in the past.

   Whether it is in the same or different organisation there will always be one 'know-all' who has been there before and will highlight the failure of similar ideas. They will be armed with a lot of negative experience, which they will introduce regardless of whether it is relevant or not. This will bring the initial upbeat tone of the idea right down. If they are feeling particularly cruel, the detractor may laugh at the idea knowingly and then ridicule it through an exaggerated story.

4. Procrastinate, delay, divert.

   These are good tactics to get the idea off the table. In the extreme the meeting may be ended because of running out of time and the idea deferred to the next meeting agenda, by which time it may be less relevant. Asking for more information can be a way of bringing the idea back to the meeting several times until it gets tired and ultimately dies.

5. Defer to another meeting.

   This may be because all the decision makers aren't in the room, or the idea doesn't fit strictly with the agenda. Moving to another meeting is likely to be met with the same resistance for the same reasons. Trying to get a specific meeting with all the right people for a single idea will prove more difficult.

6. Highlight the practical issues.

   No idea at its first hearing will have been thought through in terms of implementation. Asking a series of practical questions will de-rail the selling of the idea and leave the impression of being too difficult to do.

7. Play the legal card

    Highlight potential regulatory issues or risks about compliance and policy adherence. The more risks raised against these non-negotiable issues, the sooner people lose appetite for the idea.

8. Highlight costs and resource requirements.

    This is perhaps the most powerful way of losing support for an idea. If everyone thinks that the idea will be a threat to their own initiatives and could potentially be prioritised ahead of theirs then they will immediately turn off. Asking for people to immediately provide some resource to develop the idea will also put them off, particularly if it is before they have had a chance to understand the benefits.

9. Counter with a 'better' idea.

    In some ways this is a positive action because it could help develop the idea into something stronger. If the new idea is so off the wall that it de-rails the discussion and ultimately gets killed itself, it could absorb everyone's energy. A repeat of a few more ideas eventually loses people's attention and the conversation moves on.

10. Over praise it.

    An over enthusiastic support for the idea with all sorts of ridiculous claims about its benefits will have people challenging vehemently. The proposer will probably join in and say that some of the benefits aren't as good as being suggested and may even start doubting the idea themselves. The detractor can then agree with the proposers negative comments and the idea is dead.

It's worth considering why people like to kill ideas in order to help defend the attempt. Fundamentally, I think its fear. People are not necessarily afraid of change itself but are afraid of the threats it can bring. These threats can include:

- Ego
- Power
- Status
- Livelihood
- Career progression
- Intellect
- Familiarity
- Replacement
- Past loyalty
- Culture

If a change is represented as evolution and the journey is clearly mapped out then the understanding will be clearer. The threats should be included in the journey for an organisation and an individual. Change should be worked on at a cultural level and a personal level.

But with any change there is an upside and a risk of downside. Successful leaders of change balance the drive to achieve the vision and goals with good risk management.

Appendix F

10 successful behaviours

Appendix F
10 successful behaviours

It's often said that it is easier to teach the *right* people technical skills than it is to teach the experienced technician the right behaviours. Sometimes it's not the technical brilliance that makes the difference between success and failure. With the right personal attributes an in-experienced team can still be a success and without the right behaviour the best technicians can still fail.

The behaviours below are ones that have been highlighted as the most critical for success in change management.

1. Honesty.

    It seems obvious that everyone should be honest all of the time. But more so in programmes where big decisions can be made on the basis of small pieces of information. The classic example is whether or not people are on track. People are often reluctant to give bad news as it reflects badly on them. They may exaggerate achievements or be knowingly over optimistic with timescales and estimates in order to please. A lack of honesty will mean that the right actions can't be taken at the right time and ultimately the programme will fail in some respect.

2. Listening

    Active listening and incorporating the views of others maintains strong engagement in a change programme. This applies throughout the programme but is most commonly mentioned with regard to the managers listening to their team. Accepting bad news, challenge, estimates, and having open dialogue in how to resolve issues are all ways of demonstrating active listening.

3. Respect.

    Treat people as individuals and respect their differences. Everyone has a different level of tolerance and enthusiasm for change. It is important to consider other's positions and take time to explain why change is happening. Take time to learn where they have come from and value their past.

4. Resilience.

    This was often the single word used in answer to the question of the most important behaviour for a person delivering change. Things will inevitably go wrong during a programme and a coping mechanism and strong determination to succeed is required. People can be nurtured and helped through tough times but it is hugely helpful if they have natural resilience.

5. Challenge.

    The giving and acceptance of challenge will ensure that the right things happen for the right reasons within a programme. This occurs naturally in high performing teams but needs routine focus where it is less natural, particularly in new teams where trusted relationships haven't yet been established. How a leader responds to challenge will influence how the team acts. Role modelling a positive response and not being defensive will encourage others to challenge and increase team performance.

6. Share

    No programme can be successful without all the small parts being connected. The complex structure can soon dissolve into a chaotic mess without all elements being aligned. The sharing of accurate information is key to this. Plans, progress, estimates, designs, tests… every piece of data involved in the programme needs to be available. It is everyone's responsibility to ensure that the right people get the information they need at the time it is needed. There will be many processes and tools to help but the right behaviour is essential to make sharing the norm. Information kept to oneself is *not* power when it comes to programmes - it is a significant weakness.

7. Recognition

Leaders of teams need to understand individuals and be able to adapt to different roles and personalities. They need to be supportive when the programme is in trouble and congratulatory when there are successes. Many people in the research said that the sponsor's personal thanks was their biggest motivator. A leader needs to show interest and recognise people at the right time and in a way that motivates an individual.

8. Selflessness.

An element of competition inside a team is important but the most important team behaviour is to put the team goals ahead of the personal ones. Individual success at the expense of the bigger picture is a recipe for failure. Leaders should recognise team contribution equally to, or even higher than, achieving personal tasks.

9. Innovation.

You could argue that innovation is a skill or a natural ability rather than behaviour. The message here is that calculated risk taking is required to innovate. The right people will be able to balance the risk and benefit of an idea and act responsibly for the sake of the programme.

10. Ownership

Programme teams and individuals need to be accountable for their actions and have a desire to deliver, whatever it takes. Some people spend effort on explaining why they have failed while others put all their effort in trying to succeed. Many successful programme people don't know when to give up and have huge drive and determination to succeed, individually and for the team. This often requires a lot of flexibility in what they do and when they do it.

Appendix G

20 tips for a successful meeting

Appendix G
20 tips for a successful meeting

I hear it all the time. People are frequently complaining that they spend too much time in meetings and not enough time doing their work. This is particularly critical in change programmes, where a lot of roles are targeted and measured on low-level tasks. Meetings are an essential part of programme life and therefore it is important to get the right people at the right meeting and make them as efficient as possible.

These guidelines can be applied to most meetings as best practice, but I do acknowledge that there are many types of meetings, requiring different styles and behaviours. The guidelines can be used as a reminder for people who book, chair or attend meetings to maximise the time spent in a meeting and increase effectiveness.

The meeting guidelines can be split into 5 stages:

1. Justification

- Don't waste everyone's time by using a meeting just for presenting data or information. Simply communicating information is what memos, reports, newsletters, e-mail or phone calls are for, depending on the nature of the information and the number of recipients.

- While it is true that routine communications are essential for an effective organisation, routine meetings (those held just because it is time for another one) are not always effective. They can be major time wasters and productivity disincentives. If routine meetings do exist for good reason, often for scheduling attendance in advance, then review whether each meeting needs to occur and cancel if there isn't a good justification.

- Meetings should be called to address a specific issue or set of issues that cannot (or should not) be taken care of by an individual.

- Occasionally it would be useful to test the justification of the meeting by working out the cost of people time, location materials and preparation.

2. Planning

Whoever calls a meeting owes it to the participants to put a little planning into it:

- Prepare an e-mail announcement including a short description of the topic and a short agenda/outline of what you want to happen in the meeting, referencing or attaching any information the attendees need to review to be prepared for the meeting

- Every agenda item should have a stated objective, duration, an owner and a desired outcome.

- Pre-meeting reading should be sent well in advance of the meeting to allow time for preparation. Documents should be prepared specifically for the subject and not large amounts of data where the reader has to extract the relevant information.

- Only invite true stakeholders with regard to the subject issue. Do not be concerned about who might be offended if they are not invited, but focus on the individual's potential for contribution to the meeting. Otherwise, you will probably just be wasting their time in another boring meeting (for them).

- Hold meetings in a well-lit, well ventilated, spacious room with all the materials you may need to aid decision making e.g. white boards, flip charts, presentation equipment.

3. Presentation

- Present the central issue as concisely as possible, summarising your best understanding and analysis of all the pertinent information available. Assume everyone has read the pre-meeting material (there's nothing more annoying than spending your weekend reading and then the presenter going through the detail again).

- Stick to the agenda, avoiding the tendency to get drawn into discussions of other issues. Write down side issues on one of the boards, as topics for later discussion (if time permits) or for another meeting.

- Move as quickly as possible to the debate and action plan stage of the meeting. This is the central function of a meeting. Capture all the pertinent concerns, comments and suggestions on white boards.

4. Action

- Facilitation is everyone's responsibility. The chairperson runs the meeting and the agenda item owner facilitates their session, but it is often easier for others to observe poor meeting behaviour e.g. digression, double conversations, lack of action, time overrun, repetition, lack of listening, over-talking.

- Keep a log of decisions and actions that are visible to everyone so there are no surprises or misunderstandings after the meeting. Assign responsibilities and due dates for all action items.

- Conclude the meeting item only after some action has been agreed to, even if it is only to get more information. If an action plan cannot be agreed to, set a time to continue the meeting.

5. Follow Up

- Set a time for a follow-up meeting to review the action plan results and if necessary, do additional action planning.

- The decisions and actions should be written up immediately and sent to all attendees via e-mail.

- Keep all stakeholders (whether they attended the initial meeting or not) aware of progress on the action plan by copies of the minutes and follow-up memos. Upon successful resolution of the issue, prepare a summary report for all stakeholders, including recognition for all people who participated in accomplishing the success.

- Do a review of the meeting and solicit feedback from attendees. Document the best and worst practice in a set of guidelines for you organisation. Keep learning and improving and one day meetings will be popular.

Appendix H

20 questions

Appendix H
20 questions

This appendix describes how questionnaires were used to obtain some of the research data for the book. The best quality of information about people's experiences came from interviews but the questionnaires allowed a wider reach. There were two types of questionnaire used.

The first was based on open style questions, which encouraged freethinking, unbound by suggested answers. This is where most of the experiences come from. Respondents were encouraged to tell stories, provide anecdotes and give opinions. Some of the comments have been directly quoted in this book to illustrate a point but on the main they have been used to gain consensus on an issue. As mentioned in the introduction, the passion people have for this subject is amazing and through anonymity, not many held back. One person wrote a 3-page response to one question alone, which was probably very therapeutic for them.

Questionnaire A on the next page was sent to hundreds of people who had recently been involved in large and complex change programmes. I felt it important to strike while the iron was hot and timed the questionnaire before the post implementation reviews so there was no influence from others views and subliminally reporting on a collective response rather than their own.

The second questionnaire used more of a closed question style. Because of the multiple-choice nature of the answers I felt I could increase the number of questions and still get a good response rate. The primary output for this questionnaire was the general statements about stages of the programme cycle, based on statistical analysis. Due to its length, I haven't included it in this book.

Questionnaire B was also sent to more people and was less time dependent on where they were in the change programme cycle. Rather than recording fresh memories of a programme I was looking for results based on the experience of all programmes the respondents had been involved in during their career.

In both cases the response rate was high, more so in the more targeted Questionnaire A (over 80%) where I had the opportunity to remind (hassle) people. The cross section of respondents was also a good mix with all roles in a change programme included. These were:

- Sponsor
- Programme director
- Programme manager
- Project manager
- Consultant director
- Systems integrator director
- Business function director
- Business managers
- Business operator/agent
- IT architect
- Business architect
- IT analyst
- Business analyst
- Developer
- Tester
- Change readiness manager
- Organisation development
- Change (people) consultant
- Project office (various roles)
- Benefits manager
- Auditor

Below is the free format questionnaire. I've included it here to show the types of questions that have been asked.

A	Change Programme Management Review Questionnaire
1	What's the most important document in a change programme and why?
2	Describe your relationship with the best and worst sponsor you've worked with (no names please!). What were the impacts of the relationships on the programme?
3	Do you remember any good/bad names or vision statements for a programme you've worked on?
4	What is the best and worst example you know of an original plan versus its ultimate delivery (time or cost or scope)?
5	Can you think of an example of a design that was a stroke of genius or a disaster?
6	Do you have any good/bad examples of engaging with your programme customers?
7	What is the most important factor at the analysis/design stage? What example best demonstrates this?
8	When is it good/bad to outsource in a change programme? Do you have any examples?
9	What is the biggest thing you have learnt about how to handle people change in a programme?
10	What's usually the biggest omission in a programme and what impact does that have?
11	What's the greatest value of a project office?
12	What is the biggest programme risk that usually gets forgotten? What example best demonstrates this?
13	When should a programme be stopped before completion? Can you think of examples of programmes that should have been stopped or should have been stopped earlier?
14	What's the best and worst example of motivating the programme people that you've seen?
15	What's the most successful attribute or behaviour a person can have in a change programme.
16	Can you think of examples of good governance and bad governance?
17	What's the biggest single success factor in delivering a large and complex programme? What example best demonstrates this?
18	What's the biggest single reason that programmes fail? Can you think of a good example of failure?
18	Describe your most memorable positive project experience.
20	Describe your most memorable negative project experience.

The research hasn't stopped after publishing this book and the results are constantly being updated as I receive more stories and more data. To view or contribute to further information, please visit **www.lonelyproject.com**.

Appendix I

10 useful references

250 | Lonely Project

Appendix I
10 useful references

The main source of information for this book is the experience of change management professionals I have worked with, interviewed or have taken part in surveys. There are also other people, web sites and books that have influenced my thinking. Some are referenced in the book and others have been more of an indirect inspiration. I chose ten because if I put any more than that in, it's unlikely you'd actually look them up (I know I wouldn't). I've left out the large organisation names because, quite frankly, they don't need the plug and you probably know who they are.

1. **David Firth**. I haven't met anyone who knows more about people change than this guy, and he puts it across in simple terms and with great humour.
www.davidfirth.com

2. **Steve Myers**. An expert in team leadership development. Steve is an author, coach, mentor and deliverer of team development workshops using his own and others tools.
www.teamtechnology.com

3. **Kevin Okell.** If you're in financial services and you want to model your business to ensure you're investing in the right change… look no further.
www.altus.com

4. **Richard Hale.** A great author, inspirational coach and mentor with a real entrepreneurial spirit.
www.viprojects.com

5. **Jeff Fuge.** The best brand man I've worked with. Jeff knows how to take complex business strategies or concepts and convert them to words and pictures that people can really relate to.
www.objectiveingenuity.com

6. **Keep Walking**, Alan Chambers and Dr Richard Hale.
An inspirational story of exploration, leadership, detailed preparation, and immense determination.
www.feetofgreen.com

7. **Lend Me Your Ears**, Professor Max Atkinson.
No-nonsense delivery of how to write and deliver business presentations and public speeches. Max is an author, lecturer and personal advisor to public speakers.
www.speaking.co.uk

8. **Who Moved My Cheese?**, Dr S. Johnson.
A timeless classic book on how to survive in a changing environment… with mice!

9. **Tactics: The art of science and success**, Edward de Bono.
In a similar style to Lonely Project, this book uses research from real people who have been successful by their own definition. It extracts some learning of common characteristics of successful people.

10. **The Heart of Change**, John Kotter and Dan Cohen.
Another story-style book. It examines behaviours in changing organisations through interviewing people in the thick of change.

Appendix J

10 facts about the author

Appendix J
10 facts about the author

1. Nick Waugh has over 20 years experience of leading change.

2. He has achieved a Masters in business management, specialising in change leadership.

3. He has worked in many UK and International blue chip organisations in permanent positions and as a consultant.

4. His experience spans a number of sectors including banking, insurance, investments, manufacturing and technology.

5. He has enjoyed a variety of change programme roles that include programme director, sponsor, coach, consultant and also head of business function roles that include director of IT, change, strategy, and operations.

6. His change management style combines a pragmatic approach of re-use and proven solutions with a desire for improvement and innovation.

7. He is a non-executive director.

8. He has a network of like-minded change management professionals who he often calls upon.

9. He is a mentor and coach to people leading change.

10. He has a website where you can find a lot more.
    www.nickwaugh.co.uk